Sharing the Banquet

LITURGICAL RENEWAL IN YOUR PARISH

Sharing the Banquet

LITURGICAL RENEWAL IN YOUR PARISH

WRITTEN BY
Paul MacLean
Douglas Cowling

ILLUSTRATED BY
Jennifer Mitchell

Anglican Book Centre

1993
Anglican Book Centre
600 Jarvis Street
Toronto, Ontario
Canada M4Y 2J6

Canadian Cataloguing in Publication Data
MacLean, Paul, 1945–
    Sharing the banquet : liturgical renewal in your parish

Includes bibliographical references.
ISBN 1-55126-058-1

1.   Anglican Church of Canada – Liturgy
2.   Worship programs.   I. Cowling, Douglas.
II.   Title.

BX5616.M33 1993   264'.03   C93-094032-6

This book is dedicated
with love and affection to our families:

Sally-Beth, Avery, Conan, and Dugald
Elizabeth, John, and Aidan

Contents

Foreword

Anyone reading this book will immediately recognize the indebtedness of the authors to "a great multitude that no one can number." We have drawn ideas and inspiration from many individuals, communities, and places of worship, mostly through first-hand experience and occasionally through books. We have indicated the origins of our ideas and the process by which they have made their way into our practice in the hope that readers will be moved to similar inquisitiveness, adventure, and experimentation.

We need to mention particularly our own community of worship, St. Mary Magdalene's of Toronto, where many of the ideas presented here took practical shape. Our inspiration has been the desire to worship God in a lively fashion with this group of people, and we have been continuously helped and challenged by the many children and young people who are present.

As is the custom in a growing number of churches, we list in the service bulletin the people who have contributed to the liturgy — planners, artists, musicians, readers, dramatists, intercessors, bread bakers, greeters, servers, refreshment makers, preachers, sound system engineers.... The list often encompasses one-third of the congregation, indicating a high degree of participation and team work in the creative and mundane aspects of our liturgy. Harold Nahabedian, the rector of the parish, and Maylanne Whittall, a former honorary assistant, have participated in the process of planning and worship from the beginning and deserve special mention.

The significant contributions of all those we have worked, prayed, and played with over the last six years are reflected in the following pages and are gratefully acknowledged.

This book has been co-written. While our views are not divergent on all matters, readers may detect a certain diversity of opinion, and so we have indicated authorship of the chapters in the first two sections by the use of initials.

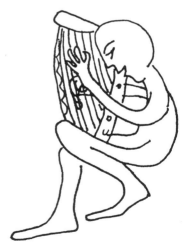

Introduction

There is a new church in our midst. It has been created by the Holy Spirit. We can see its signs in many forms. This church is struggling to express itself, and the language and forms of worship available are those of an older church. These two churches, old and new, exist together, sometimes worshipping in the same building but in separate congregations, sometimes in hostile and exclusive liturgies, sometimes in a negotiated compromise in a single congregation, often in an uneasy equilibrium within a single individual.

The signs of the new church have been remarked upon in many publications about theology, church, and liturgy. There is the creative energy released by the Second Vatican Council which has affected all Christian traditions. Similarly, the various renewal movements including the charismatic movement have known no denominational boundaries and have brought profound changes to the spirit of worship. Feminism has had its influence on the church, showing that the Holy Spirit works from outside as well as within the church. A movement with its beginning in the early days of the World Council of Churches, lay ministry, now renamed in some quarters as baptismal ministry, has reclaimed the biblical notion of the whole people of God being a royal priesthood. Concern for issues of justice and ecology, while not limited to the new church, help to shape its ethos. Liberation themes such as solidarity with people enslaved, whether by oppressive regimes in the third world or addictions in the first or poverty in both, have helped to create the new church. Finally, there has been a growing movement to acknowledge children and young people as full members of the Christian community.

The new church is more than a renewal of the old. It is also composed of people who are coming to faith as adults and who are discovering or perhaps naming the mysterious presence of God for the first time. These people are often referred to as the unchurched or those with no Christian memory. Coming with enthusiasm but little tradition, they need the gifts of the old church as well as the new for their spiritual lives.

The new church exists in a world and society far different from that which shaped the old church. In North America we are now a society which is pluralistic. The old attitudes which included at least an assumption of superiority relating to race, religion, and tradition are no longer adequate. We are called to exist within and respond to a world which is interdependent in all its aspects: ecologically, economically, socially, and on a simple human scale. The world is in crisis because its interdependent relationships are ignored.

"How do we sing the Lord's song in a strange land?" wrote a psalmist during the exile of Israel in Babylon. We are in a position in which the land is strange, the ancient songs and liturgies at our disposal are too antiquated for contemporary religious discourse, and those of us who want to sing are still discovering who we are and what God has in mind for us.

There are in fact many voices that have helped the new church find its acts of praise. The acts of praise are authentic and powerful words with which to address God and raise up to the Creator the cry of creation. They are songs which evoke the faithful and loving acts of God for this place and time.

—PM

* * *

The reflections and suggestions which have shaped much of our thoughts about liturgy have come primarily from our practical experiences at a small church in downtown Toronto. St. Mary Magdalene's is an Anglican parish with a strong liturgical life in the catholic tradition. Although it is well known for its musical tradition established under Healey Willan, the parish's chief mission has always been the renewal of the eucharistic life of its parishioners and of the wider Anglican church in Canada. With that sacramental commitment at its core, the parish has also faced the same issues which the church at large faces. And like other communities, the parish has responded differently at different times. On some issues — most notably the recognition of women's ministries — the progress has been glacial. On the other hand, St. Mary Magdalene's has also been committed to an ongoing liturgical experiment.

Two important events should be noted that are part of the personal profile of this faith community. Over 20 years ago, Eugene Fairweather, the noted theologian and a long-time assistant priest in the parish, established the pattern of a monthly eucharist at 9:30 A.M. which tried to involve the children in the liturgy in a very direct way. The children read the lessons, led the intercessions, were the servers, and brought up the offertory. At the beginning, the rite was traditional, but over the years the "folk mass" has experimented with and moved to contemporary language and music. That continuing commitment to the involvement of children in the liturgy remains a significant achievement for the parish and an invaluable base from which to explore the wider possibilities for inclusive worship. We have been blessed with talented, dedicated people, and our freedom to experiment is based in a well-loved tradition which expects and encourages young people's participation in the liturgy.

The second factor which has had a profound effect on the parish has been the most recent theological thinking which views baptism as full incorporation as a member of the church. This trend meant a re-evaluation of our practice of admitting children to communion. If baptism made them full and equal partners in the church, how could we deny them the bread and cup? After much discussion and a number of programs, the parish gradually came to the collective understanding that the table was open to all Christians and that children of all ages were welcome. In many churches, this discussion continues and may not be resolved immediately. In our community, however, we have found that the open table is both an encouragement to young families and an exciting challenge to the other parishioners. The sight of two-year-olds munching on the bread, and infants sucking a finger dipped in the wine has dramatically brought home our obligation to nurture the spiritual formation of all our members. More significantly, we have discovered that adults as well as children are hungering for a new experience of the liturgy. We remain bemused and amused by the enthusiasm which adults display for activities supposedly designed for young people. What began as a focussed children's liturgy has evolved into a more inclusive worship experience which sees the power of symbols, music, and movement for all ages.

Having said that, it should be noted that we are also the sum of our limitations. We continue to face the same problems with resources that every community faces. For every successful liturgy outlined here, there is another which did not take place because we didn't have adequate time, personnel, expertise, money, or energy. An important part of our liturgical planning has been a growing realization that we simply can't import a liturgy from another setting or from a book about liturgy. Ultimately, our liturgies must rise from the people who celebrate them. The experiences of other faith communities have much to give us, and we should always be looking and listening and praying with them. But in the final analysis, a true *eucharistia,* a true *thanksgiving,* is animated and illuminated by the community itself.

This is not liturgical trendiness: we are not concocting liturgical entertainment for the television generation, or sentimentalizing worship so that it is "relevant." It seems to us that the flexibility to experiment must come out of a regular worship experience which is evolving and growing in a slower, perhaps more natural, way. All of the liturgies in this book are "occasional" liturgies in our parish: they are offered once a month; the other three weeks are given over to quite a conservative, normative service. The frustration often encountered with the "traditional" liturgy is balanced with a thankfulness that week after week it continues to feed us and that men and women are pouring hard work and love into its celebration. We have to take care of the valleys as well as the mountain tops.

For some, this book may seem surprisingly conservative. Many readers will want a "clean-slate" approach to worship where everything is created afresh each time. Our experience has suggested that the most enduring liturgical renewal has taken place in communities where continuity and tradition have been renewed and restored. Yes, there are certainly times for a prophetic "shock of the new," but it is almost impossible to sustain relentless novelty merely because of dissatisfaction with what came before. To us, the real radical change comes in looking at the familiar or the mandated or the expected with a new perspective. We take a reading, an action, a symbol, an event, and ask, "What is this? ... How is God speaking to us through this? ... How can we respond to this?" That process can ignite a revolution in thinking. Sometimes the response is new; sometimes it is the familiar revivified.

The authors should also admit that they are confirmed church rats, and whenever travelling can usually be found dragging their families to the local interesting liturgy. Once back home some of our planning time is given over to debriefing these worship experiences with the rest of our planning team. Whether it is a base community in Mexico, a Benedictine monastery in France, or a parish in Ontario cottage country, our discussion tends to focus on the question, "What quality or principle made that a GOOD liturgy?" It's not a question of how we could reproduce a particular event in our own church; rather, it's an attempt to discover the underlying commonality of the religious impulse. This process of reflection has proved to be one of our most important tools for liturgy. Nor are the authors always in agreement. A close interlinear translation of this book will disclose unresolved questions and different perspectives. We have not tried to homogenize our thoughts or styles. The observations and suggestions offered here are primarily impressions based on experience: they are not intended as a systematic commentary on the new rites, nor as a programmed strategy for liturgical change.

In practical terms, this book is speaking to people who love their particular church or community, and want more for it. For some, it may be a means of drawing in new members; for most, it will be a continuing need to renew the faith of present members. More particularly, the book is intended to promote discussion and self-examination within a congregation. The last thing we intend is that the observations and suggestions offered here are instant recipes for success — that all you have to do is slap this page on the photocopier and you have a sure-fire winner. To be perfectly honest, our planning does not produce slick, seamless liturgies. We have plenty of bumps along the way, and during the liturgy there are plenty of mistakes and miscalculations. *Liturgy* means the work: the work of the people of God. It is demanding, frustrating, exhausting work. What we also say is that the liturgy is a work of joy and wonder.

—DC

Exploring

Resources

"The Spirit of the Lord is upon me, because he has anointed me to preach good news to the poor. He has sent me to proclaim release to the captives and recovering of sight to the blind, to set at liberty those who are oppressed, to proclaim the acceptable year of the Lord" (Luke 4:18–19, quoted from Isaiah 61:1–2 and 58:6).

We were a gathering of about 200 in the rectangular hall, seated in an oval about five rows deep. This was the weekly eucharist, held for the summer-session students at Boston College, a Roman Catholic university with faculties in arts, science, and theology. Unlike on other occasions, no books or leaflets were handed out, but we were soon engaged in learning a musical setting for the Lucan passage quoted above. These verses formed an introductory canticle of great energy, at the end of which a priest, dressed in a simple chausuble, stepped into the centre of the oval, said the collect for the day, and then we all sat down.

With the next episode it became apparent that, much like theatre in the round, we were defining the liturgical space by our oval. Someone emerged from the congregation and uttered a short passage from Isaiah in much the same way an actor would deliver a speech to an audience. In quick succession, an African stood in the centre and told us what the prophet's words meant to someone who lived daily with oppression and poverty; an American spoke on their meaning for a member of the suburban middle class; another signed the passage for the deaf with beautiful, fluid movements; and a young dancer gave a simple and graceful interpretation. Each of these reflections on the prophet's declamation was separated by silence and then the sung refrain which had begun the liturgy, acting as a sort of antiphon. Taken together, the various pieces of spoken words, bodily movements, stillness and music built on each other to create a rich and powerful effect. The prophetic word was heard and felt in many dimensions.

Surprisingly there were no intercessions, but next we were invited to exchange the peace as a symbolic act of solidarity with those who suffered. The music began, a more complex variation of our opening canticle, and miraculously a table appeared in our midst replete with bread and wine. The celebrant appeared and sang a eucharistic prayer (composed, I suspect, on the spot), punctuated by a lusty refrain. We communicated each other with words drawn from the Lucan theme. Then some minutes of silence during which we spoke a word or phrase of intercession or thanksgiving. Dismissal.

Reflecting on this eucharist, I realized that the printed word had been completely absent. Not a single piece of paper or book had been used by anyone. With a minimum of musical coaching and a remembered tradition of basic eucharistic elements we had all the resources we needed for our full participation. In fact, the removal of our familiar props sharpened our attention and increased our participation. Furthermore, the resources for the presentation of the eucharist had been drawn from the abilities and experience of the community — music, speech, theological reflection, dance, signing, and a liberal dash of imagination and liturgical sense contributed by the planning team. These contributions were all intensely human and, although in some cases and to some degree they required specialist ability, they were all easily accessible and appreciated by the congregation.

Before drawing out some of the learnings from this eucharist for the practice of liturgies in a more general sense, it would be advisable to state its particularities. The congregation for whom the eucharist was planned were summer-school students, many of whom were enrolled in religious education courses. They were therefore a specialized group who were learning together and probably more open than most to liturgical innovation. It would be an unusual congregation that would accept this liturgy as its weekly act of worship. However, the liturgy was entirely appropriate in its setting and was a vehicle for the lifting up of hearts and voices to the God who "lifts the poor out of the mire." Also, with care some of the ideas present in this liturgy may be adapted to other settings.

There is a more general question which this liturgy articulates, and which has relevance for all liturgical planning. What resources are necessary for the presentation of liturgy? Congregations have been held captive by unexamined models which demand resources the average congregation is unable to muster. Music is perhaps the best example. Countless Anglican congregations have in the past struggled to imitate the repertoire and standards of English cathedral and college choirs without notable success. More appropriate models were certainly lacking, but also the exploration of musical resources within the congregation and wider community was rarely under-taken. Trombones and flutes, after all, didn't fit into the accepted model for liturgical music.

I remember stumbling into a packed church one Sunday morning in the south of France to the unfamiliar sounds of organ, saxophone, flute, and drums. The organist also happened to be the leader of a jazz group, and had composed a jazz mass which had been enthusiastically adopted by the congregation (it must be added, adopted over the protests of the priest who favoured a more traditional form of music ap-proved by the ecclesiastical authorities). This was a church which had not been captive to the officially endorsed models of mass settings, and had developed its own indigenous tradition, using the musical resources at hand.

Two more examples will expand this point about making the best use of the resources that are present within a community. I once attended a service in an English town on the recommendation that the vicar had a particularly effective ministry. It transpired that the vicar was on holiday, that the service was morning prayer from *The Book of Common Prayer* (1662) conducted entirely by members of the congregation, and that the oldest member of our family was younger by at least a generation than the next youngest member of the congregation. Yet the effectiveness of ministry was transparently clear. The sermon was excellent and the reading of David's lament over the death of Jonathan by an elderly gentleman was so moving that our small children were transfixed. More could be said about this memorable matins, but the overall impression that remained for me was of human resources being intelligently developed and employed for the purposes of worship and building of community. What could so easily be dismissed — an older congregation, the old prayer book, amateur leadership — in fact was all turned to advantage. The absent vicar probably had something to do with bringing out the gifts of the congregation.

The third example comes from a small, poor French village in the heart of a popular tourist region. The church building was in thorough disrepair and was bare except for an altar and wooden benches. The parish priest was an engaging, charismatic man who visited enthusiastically with the holiday makers. Sunday mass found a full church building, so full that we had to sit on a bench behind the altar. What resources were evident in the presentation of this eucharist when there was so little to draw upon? First, the priest had engaged the services of a young flautist who played a simple prelude and postlude. Second, visual images appropriate to the readings for the day — a sheaf of wheat from the nearby fields and an icon — were placed prominently on the altar. Third, we were taught some simple music to sing at several points in the liturgy. Seldom have I seen so few resources used to such good effect. There was not even a local tradition to draw upon because most of the congregation were present for the first and only time. We vacationers had been drawn together to celebrate the mystery of our redemption and re-creation by the energy and imagination of a priest who knew that the love of God, the story of Jesus, a small amount of bread and wine were all the resources necessary.

The resources for liturgy are to be found primarily within people, both clergy and laity. The leadership which plans a liturgy for a congregation should have a clear idea of liturgical purpose and shape and the elements which normally go into making up a liturgy. The leaders should also look first to the people in the congregation and wider community if they want the liturgy to be both of and for the people. Such indigenous liturgy is also probably a more authentic offering of worship to God than worship which simply follows a prescription from elsewhere.

Keeping in mind the principle of people first establishes two things. First, it unlocks the vast potential that exists in even the smallest congregation for effective proclamation, musical variety, visual imagination, heart-felt intercession, and the building of diverse community. Second, it releases us from the tyranny of liturgical forms, whether contained in books or in grand traditions. We can regard these forms and traditions for what they are, that is, valuable secondary resources which we adapt to our settings to assist the gathered people of God in their worship.

—PM

The Whole Worshipper

"Look at that," the mother of a five year old sighed, "He's drawn another dinosaur."

We had all been asked to help decorate a large Easter card for a visiting bishop: "Please draw a symbol of what worship means to you." Most of us had dutifully drawn joined hands, crosses, cups.... But there among the predictable symbols was a fiercely unchurched dinosaur. For a moment we speculated how the activity had gone awry. A secular picture had intruded on our sacred symbols — the religious exercise had become mere play.

We then remembered that the dinosaur had appeared before — in Advent. A potter had come to explore the theme of God the Creator — "You are the potter; we are the clay" was the reading. The children had plunged their hands into wet clay and created passionate images of life: birds, people, dogs ... and a dinosaur. And now during the Easter celebration of new life, our five-year-old creator had taken his dinosaur and raised it from extinction and death. A new symbol of Easter had been born.

We almost missed that new symbol. We had expected something familiar, something "appropriate." We had narrowed our religious sensibilities so that we failed to recognize that from those dirty hands and the crucible of that individual's experience could come a "God-bearing" symbol.

Our worship is impoverished by that failure.

However, our encounter with the Lord of the Dinosaurs can give us fresh insights into this dilemma.

First, children experience their world through a totality of their senses. Touch, taste, smell, sight, and hearing are all avenues of exploration for feelings and ideas. Adults often do not even hear or feel many sensory stimuli until they have them pointed out by a child. The directness of children's responses is so powerful that adults can even worry about over-stimulation.

Second, children interpret their world through their own perspective. Adults are constantly delighted and bewildered by the freedom and creativity with which children see the world. Through the prism of their own lives, they see larger patterns when adults are obsessed with details; they see the small and particular when others see only the big picture.

In short, children are ready to accept the transforming grace of God because they do not close the countless doors and windows through which the transcendent can break into their lives.

What does this tell us about worship?

As we pass through childhood and adolescence into adulthood, we give the greatest weight to rational, logical processes. We therefore train ourselves to regard religion as essentially an intellectual exercise: we consider various statements of belief, assess them, and then make a decision to assent or dissent. As adults, we do not trust our senses — even the adjectives *sensual* or *sensuous* carry negative connotations. And yet the eucharist is primarily a thing which is *done* — "Do this in memory of me," not "*Read* this." Most of us primarily think of worship as a series of texts. When the words are chosen, the preparation is over. Great texts may be read, great prayers recited, and great sermons preached, but we still hear the criticism that worshippers do not feel involved in the liturgy, or that they want more active participation.

Perhaps we should become as little children for a moment and look at some of the elements of our communal religious experience. In all of the following situations, the religious response of the worshipper was visceral, not intellectual. The liturgy was felt.

* * *

At one inter-generational eucharist, we wanted the children to feel more involved in the Great Thanksgiving, that long, long prayer of consecration. So we asked them to play Orff instruments for the acclamation, "Glory to you for ever and ever," which recurs throughout that particular prayer. The instruments were all percussion: xylophones, glockenspiel, wood blocks, bells — irresistible to children.

The celebrant began the prayer which proclaims God's saving work in the creation, redemption, and sanctification of the world. After each section, the children's instruments rang out with amazing power. Their brows furrowed as they concentrated hard on their miniature melodies; the adults grinned at such tuneful harmony for their singing. The back-and-forth rhythm of proclamation and acclamation moved one youngster in particular. After each instrumental chorus, he would drop his percussion sticks, race behind a pillar, and improvise an ecstatic but silent little dance. Then, without any adult prompting, he would run back to his xylophone to be ready for the first note of the next chorus.

That child's actions, which again could have been misinterpreted as mere play, tell us a great deal about the power of music in worship. On one hand, it was deeply communal. Without listening and responding to each other, the children could not create harmony. On the other hand, the music gave an opportunity for an improvisation as exciting as a jazz solo or an organ postlude. Above all, the child was entering into the rhythm of story and response which is the essence of our Great Thanksgiving. The response was physical, the movement of bone and muscle.

We adults have lost the physicality of music. For the most part, European and North American culture have given up all direct music-making, whether sacred or secular. We have handed over the singing and playing to the professionals, and are passively content to listen. The great achievements of Western European music should not blind us to the equally great sacrifices which we have had to make. We have given up the extraordinary bonds which music creates in a community. And we have given up the physical sensations of breathing and moving which are experienced by both classical musicians and village drummers.

We live in a culture where there is a great deal of music but very little music-making. The difference between children and adults is striking. As children, we make rhythm and song integral components of our play; as adults, we say that we love music but are not musical. Perhaps one of the last vestiges of our lost musicality is

"Happy Birthday to You." The rite of blowing out the candles on the cake is simply impossible without the song. It is a musical symbol which expresses the whole mind and heart of the celebrating community.

The experience of non-Western Christians is helpful here. In cultures where music demands active communal participation, there is no problem with involvement. In fact, most cannot conceive of a said service — music is an integral part of religious experience. We should pause to assert that we are not promoting any particular style of music. The point is rather that the experience of music requires participation. The rhythm of worship is the rhythm of music. And through the harmony of community and the song of individuals, we open ourselves to the richest gifts of the Spirit.

* * *

The children were painting a rainbow.

Around the canvas banner were pie-plates full of primary colours as irresistible as the bells and glockenspiels. The children knew what to do instinctively: they dipped their hands enthusiastically into the paint and created the bands of the rainbow with handprints. God's covenant with all the peoples of the world.

When she thought that no one was looking, one mother slipped her hand into the yellow paint and surreptitiously planted her handprint among the children's. She looked a little sheepish when we spotted her. She laughed and held out a brilliant yellow hand in explanation, "I'd forgotten how it felt to fingerpaint: I wanted to be part of the banner."

If our culture allows us little music, it allows us less art.

Our fingerpainting mother was trying to reclaim something which she hardly realized had been taken away from her: the feeling of colour and shape and texture between her fingers. One of the joys of the artist is the tactile quality of the media: the hardness of the stone, the shapelessness of the clay, the viscosity of the paint. Children delight in their media. In fact, some children do not produce a "work of art" at all; they are quite content with simply touching and playing with the materials.

So too the rhythm of art. Young children often make repetitive pictures through a simple enjoyment of repetitive motion: drawing circles, filling a space with dots, scribbling lines across a page. Again, the sheer physicality stimulates the imagination and the emotions.

As adults, unless we are self-proclaimed artists, we have been desensitized to the tactile, kinesthetic joys of art. Our mother with the yellow hand realized that she had given up a pleasurable creative activity in the process of growing up. But she also wanted to be part of the meaning of the banner. She wanted her handprint to make her part of the rainbow, part of God's covenant.

Children have powerful symbolic systems. Their favourite colours and their vivid dreams display a rich visual imagination which helps interpret the world to them, and themselves to the world. Some images may be incomprehensible to us; others may have a deep resonance in our communal experience. Children understand those extremes. They will acknowledge and tolerate the image which has a private meaning, but more importantly, they will take possession of a symbol which speaks to their own experience. They will not hesitate to be part of the rainbow.

But are we ready to accept a dinosaur as a religious symbol?

If we have become passive listeners of music, we have surely become passive viewers of an art with a narrow range of meanings. The colours of the church year have been codified and a fairly clear line has been drawn between sacred and secular art. By systematizing our symbols, we have lost our ability to create new symbols which could speak with a new eloquence to our present lives. Those new symbols rise only through dirty hands and liberated imaginations.

* * *

Something was going wrong at the children's eucharist.

The pews couldn't hold them — they were everywhere: peering behind the altar, walking in the aisles, stacking up the books. The entire church seemed to be a sea of movement and — yes, let's admit it — noise! When "Go in peace!" was finally shouted over the din, the adult interpretation of the event began. One school of thought maintained that we had passed THE LIMIT: there was so much activity that nothing could be heard or understood. Another school was moved by the chaos: the children felt comfortable and secure enough to be themselves.

The planning group scratched its head over the response, but slowly realized that the liturgy had sent a mixed message to the children. We had planned to ask them to move to three successive locations in the church, where they would encounter a different reading dramatized in a different way: Isaiah's vision of heaven was staged in the sanctuary with thunderous music and clouds of incense, Paul's tender picture of God's adoption of us was read from a rocking chair at the font, and Nicodemus's visit to Jesus was re-enacted in the nave with a former school administrator as the inquirer and a teenage student as the teaching Master. The movement from one location to another created a rhythm of standing and moving, of solo and chorus, as we explored the boundaries of the liturgical space. By keeping the entire congregation in motion, we realized that we had inadvertently asked them to dance. Little wonder that they could not stand still for the rest of the eucharist!

Movement and dance seem to appear spontaneously in children's play. We should keep our notion of dance as wide as possible at this point. Rhythmic play to songs or poetry are obviously part of dance. But if dance is movement which creates recurring patterns within a space and within time, then we must include sports in the phenomenon. For most children, adult distinctions between work and play, or the arts and sports, or movement and dance are meaningless.

Dance is a claiming of a space. When our over-eager worshippers crawled under the altar, they were touching and making the building their own as surely as a dance troupe takes possession of a stage. Children take the space which they need for their play. If it is too big, they will establish their own limits; if it is too small, they will push the limits. Their playing space always seems to have a wonderful appropriateness, whether it is as intimate as cushions piled in a chair or as expansive as a playground. The power of place is undeniable: victims of the Holocaust recall with wonder that children in the death camp of Auschwitz were still able to create their own playing space even in the midst of a place that seemed beyond time and place.

We adults often feel awkward in spaces that are not familiar or which we cannot control. Our complex construct of territoriality can paralyze us into inactivity at times. We have lost the ability to claim our space through movement: we cannot dance the ground any longer.

* * *

"And they made a crown of thorns.... "

The Palm Sunday reading of the passion story was being acted out by the children. We simply couldn't manage a costumed drama, so we fell back on the traditional division of speeches among various readers. We asked the children to bring up the symbols as they appeared in the story: a purple cloak, a cup, a burial sheet. A six year old came forward with a vine twisted into a circlet. Like the others, he showed his symbol to the congregation. But then, unprompted, he raised his hand in a gesture of such utter sadness and helplessness that for a moment we were there in Jerusalem, experiencing Jesus' loneliness and pain. The action had ceased to be a mere re-enactment or memorial: it had become real in the hearts and minds of the onlookers.

That new reality, that drama, is a constant feature of children's play. They create characters, actions, and emotions that are real. The parents of highly imaginative children often worry that they are in another world. And like all great dramatists, children want to share their new reality with others. There are no greater moments for adults than to be invited into the dynamic play world of children. The sense of delight and recognition is unforgettable.

For most of us, drama has become a segregated activity characterized by over-priced tickets and uncomfortable theatre seats. The liturgy can give us back some of the communal experience of another reality: that is the hallmark of drama. Emotions, ideas, personalities come to us in a new reality. Some people speak of the way in which friends and family who have died seem to stand with us at communion time. Or the way in which a "call" to a particular ministry seemed as strong as if a voice had spoken. These are not sentimental or neurotic experiences: they are new dramatic realities, they are encounters with the risen Christ.

But does all this sensory activity belong to Christian worship? Isn't the Christian liturgy essentially an activity of the mind, something spiritual?

The precedents for hands-on liturgy can be found in all traditions: the drums and dancing of the Coptic church, the liturgical drama of medieval England, the dancing choirboys of Seville Cathedral, the circle procession of the Greek Orthodox wedding ... the historical evidence is there if we care to look for it. It isn't always in the main-stream, but it is there as a constant impulse in Christian tradition.

But isn't this all too much like the "throwaway" culture? Children's paintings and plays ... aren't we throwing out the great history of Western art, poetry, and music: the Sistine Chapel, Handel's *Messiah*, the poetry of T.S. Eliot? Those wonderful artifacts will always be part of our tradition if we love them. But we cannot depend on them alone to inform our worship. We have to be prepared to expand beyond the narrow confines of five or six centuries of Western European experience. Liturgical renewal is not just a question of texts or artistic monuments: it is a realignment of the whole person towards the saving activity of Christ. And in the course of our encounter we will have experiences which are not great art, which will not require guide books in a hundred years.

We have to trust that the Spirit will speak to us through those dirty hands, those torn pieces of newsprint, and those mumbling voices.

We have to *do* it in memory of him.

—DC

Symbols

A group of 20 children sat in front of the altar, surrounding the celebrant. Their attention was drawn to a large clay pot. "Can you guess what is inside?" Wild and inaccurate responses. Investigation. There were thousands of sunflower seeds. The children transferred the seeds to baskets and then circulated them to the congregation. "Could everyone hold a seed in their hand? Now close your eyes. Can you feel it in your hand? What is it like? Can you think of anything else as light and as small as this seed?" More wild responses. "Ah, but this seed is different. It will turn into something if you plant it in the ground. It will become a wonderful plant, taller than anyone here."

The celebrant continued: "There are many wonderful things that begin as tiny seeds. Do you see baby Nathaniel, sitting on his daddy's knee? You remember how tiny he was when he was baptised? Look how much he has grown! Well, he began as a little seed inside his mummy's tummy, just like each of you, and look how big you are now.

"Did you know that a very wise woman a long time ago called Julian held in her hand a nut, which is a seed that will grow into a tree. She said as she held that nut, that she was holding everything in the whole world. I think she knew that God makes everything in the world, and that God makes wonderful things from the tiniest beginnings.

"Jesus told a story about God creating a wonderful kingdom from very small beginnings. People were very sad and depressed because they wanted God's kingdom to come right away and they couldn't see any signs that it was happening. So Jesus said, 'God's kingdom is like a tiny seed that grows into a great bush, so big that even birds are able to build their nests in it.' He was thinking about the birds because he knew that God's kingdom is big enough to have a special place for everybody.

"Now let's look at our seeds. Who can tell me what they will look like when they have grown into flowers? If four of you will help, you will be able to see what a beautiful garden your tiny seeds will become."

Then, a large green canvas was unfolded to reveal a three-dimensional display of sunflowers, and this was attached to the altar. After some moments of admiration and comment, the children were invited to think of a prayer. As they made their prayer, they placed their seed in one of several pots of earth at the base of the sunflower garden. The rest of the congregation joined in with their intercessions after this beginning to complete the prayers of the people.

This is an example of a contextual symbol shaping a homily and introducing an act of intercession. By contrast here is an account of the use of a modern sign.

The homilist wished to illustrate the operation of the Holy Spirit through human beings. He engaged a group of children in a series of magnetic experiments. The magnet not only attracted various bits of metal, but those bits which were attracted in turn attracted others so long as they remained attached to the magnet. The homiletic point was made that as long as we remain in God's love we are able to share that love with others. Many of the intricacies of John 17 became clearer to children and adults alike.

Although these homilies seem on the surface to be similar in that they both make use of concrete objects, there is in fact a major difference between them which stems from the nature of the objects from which they derive their separate meanings. The magnet is a sign. It has no relation to the Holy Spirit as such, but through the imagination of the homilist its properties of force and attraction are used to illustrate similar spiritual realities. The magnetic forces in themselves are not part of these spiritual realities. On the other hand, the seed takes part in the miraculous process of growth by which something very small becomes wonderfully large. In addition to being part of a larger reality to which it points, the seed evokes a host of similar examples even in young children: human beings, such as themselves, have their beginnings as small seeds and become wonderfully complex and capacious creatures, able to embrace vast networks of knowledge and a great diversity of human communities.

Signs are useful for imparting straightforward information and for explaining or simplifying things. Symbols at their best hold within themselves many layers of meaning and make connections between those layers even if at an unconscious level. With children there is a simple evoking of awe at something so small becoming magnificently large. But the adults who allow themselves to meditate on the meaning of the seed in their hands find a host of associations adhering to this tiny object. Religious meaning is found both in the awe and wonder that comes naturally to small children and in the more adult connections made through symbolic association between the many and varied experiences of the creative process.

Some writers will use the terms *sign* and *symbol,* but with different meanings from the definitions and distinctions being employed here. For example, the Gospel of John speaks of signs performed by Jesus; yet these signs clearly have all the characteristics of what we mean by symbols. Even if there is not total agreement on the use of the two terms, the underlying distinction between the two meanings is important to maintain.

Religion is primarily concerned with symbolic meaning. Through symbols we make connections between our lives and transcendent reality. To call something "just a symbol" means for that person the something is operating only as a sign. Once the information is grasped or the concept explained, the object can be discarded without violating the reality to which it points. Magnets can be put back in the pocket, but there would have been an outcry if the seeds did not have a decent burial. (Disposal through eating also has noble precedents, but this activity was not encouraged.)

The way in which we explore symbols is very different from the use of signs. Signs must be bold and obvious. Symbols are often parts of our everyday life, yet they must be explored with a sense of anticipation that within them there is much to be discovered. Grains of mustard seed turning into small trees are simply not part of our experience: to use mustard seeds would have been bewildering as well as botanically inaccurate. But most of us have had some experience of sunflower seeds, and perhaps there is a similar reaction to the extraordinary flowers they produce as the reaction Jesus intended for his listeners when they gazed on a Mediterranean bush large enough for birds to nest in. Within that small seed held in a hand there were many things to be discovered and connections to be made. Sometimes we need the confidence to stay with a symbol and explore its meaning instead of looking only for what is superficially obvious and rushing on to another image.

Research in human development has revealed that symbols are powerful forces for ordering experience from a very early age. Stories perform this function in later childhood once a child is able to comprehend the passage of time. When intellectual capacities develop further, abstract thought provides the structure for making sense of life. However, just as stories do not lose their power to convey meaning in adulthood, so symbols remain with us all our lives like the outer rings of a tree. Symbols are a common ground for all ages, although the meaning they convey will obviously vary according to the developmental stage. Furthermore, a symbol which makes a vivid impression in childhood will likely remain a source of strength throughout that person's life.

In her book, *The Religious Potential of the Child*, (p. 166) Sophia Cavalletti writes of an experience of the symbol of light with young children. In response to the light of a baptismal candle, given by God, the children reflect, "that we are small," "that we are good," "that God is good," and "that we are great." Cavalletti comments, "Humility and wonder are two interrelated attitudes ... the signs, whose meaning will never be depleted, are instruments, without substitute, to keep alive that emotion which ... is proper to the child and has such importance in the *homo religiosus."* In her book, Cavalletti derives the term *sign* from the Gospel of John, but in this context its meaning is identical to the word *symbol* which we have been using. This gospel is the richest source of symbols in the New Testament, containing at least 39. She goes on to say that teaching through symbols produces the attitude of humility in both child and adult, because symbols are always allusive and never depleted of their meaning. "Face to face with the unfathomability of the Christian message and its inexhaustible richness, the person will feel small and great: small in front of the infinite Mystery; great, because it has been given to him to enter it in some way, great with a greatness that is gift."

To be small and great at one and the same time is the religious experience of holding a tiny seed in one's hand.

To compare again the seed and the magnet: why is one a symbol and the other a sign? Does a symbol have to come from the world of nature and have within it the potential for creativity? Are objects associated with science always relegated to the status of signs? Certainly a mechanistic view of the world has no place in it for symbols. Some would argue that the dominance of science as a way of explaining the world has been one of the chief reasons for the decline in the importance of symbols for ordering our experience. We seek our explanations in facts, not allusions. With science explaining everything from nature to economics, religion is reduced to a privatized sphere and religious symbols are tame and domesticated.

The religious spirit seeks a unified view of the world, and is not content with catering to a small, personal part of human life. So too, religious symbols are attempts to achieve some form of unity, bringing together many disparate aspects of human experience, the world, and God. But if the observation about the influence of the scientific world view is correct, then it means that there are not a large number of potent religious symbols at hand which will convey meaning in our present age. It is a task of liturgy to discover symbols that do have meaning. In some cases this can be achieved by unearthing the hidden possibilities within traditional symbols, bringing new life to them. In other instances we need to be more daring and experimental, running the risk that the symbols we choose will be ephemeral and not carry the weight of religious significance we intend; but drawing back if our experiments lead to silliness.

Here are only two examples of traditional symbols that could use some rediscovery. Blood is one of the most powerful symbols in all human cultures, yet despite its arresting presence in the Old and New Testaments and in modern culture, we seem to shy away from using it in church. Similarly, sex is not much mentioned in our churches for its positive symbolic value, as if we are too afraid of its destructive power. Yet it is a great creative force and one of the chief images in the bible for the relations between God and humanity. The references to our common origin as seeds and to the presence of a baby were simple ways of drawing attention to the symbolic or sacramental power of sex. Family is another related symbol that has great potential for connecting and giving meaning to the various communities of which we are a part. However, it needs to be freed from the limited and sometimes oppressive associations with the idealized nuclear families of Western societies.

Liturgy is concerned with the creative use of symbols. They can't be invented, but they can be discovered. In this task artists are essential to liturgical planning and execution, because they have experience and expertise in reading and exploring the meaning of the symbols by which our culture defines itself. We can also learn from the example of artists who explore the music and art of other cultures to find new and invigorating emotions and forms. If our liturgies are to come to life, then we shall have to take some risks in experimenting with new symbols, to see if they will help us make religious meaning of our lives.

A more balanced view of modern science than the stereotype presented above would recognize the tremendous advances in quantum and particle theory as gifts to the human imagination to comprehend the macrocosm and microcosm of our existence. Science may well provide us with a new source of symbols. If that magnet were to be presented as a symbolic embodiment of the force field surrounding the globe, affecting the northern lights, giving directions to compasses, reflecting the creative order by which the universe was formed....

—PM

Expanding & Including

On a bright, sunny Sunday morning we were driven through the labyrinth of streets that makes up Mexico City and arrived at a building looking like every other building we had passed, that is to say about the size and in the dilapidated condition of my garage in Toronto. This was church, the meeting place for worship of about 40 members of all ages of a Mennonite congregation. We were a group of six visitors from as many countries, all in Mexico for a meeting of the World Council of Churches. It was the practice of the WCC on such occasions to disperse its international committee members to local congregations for interchanges which were undoubtedly surprising to both parties.

Our only expectation of the service was that one of our members — a bishop from the Caribbean — would preach. However, as the service began, our interpreter gently but firmly indicated the wishes of the Mennonite pastor that all of us would speak the word of the Lord. Feeling a strong bond of sympathy for the young children present and contemplating the number of sermons they had in store, I resolved to teach them a song as my contribution to the preaching marathon. As it turned out my comrades had similar thoughts and came up with stories and songs to share with the congregation. Just as well, because the pastor had his own prepared sermon to deliver and a member of the congregation suddenly felt moved to speak at some length too.

Our inadequate facility with Spanish prevented us from understanding and engaging fully in the service. However, I thought that the hymns we were singing were all distantly familiar. They were Spanish hymns, but the cursillo movement had spread them throughout the world and given Christians a common language of praise.

The sermon-laden liturgy ended, but the experience of church continued for another four hours in the little courtyard adjacent to the building. Here we ate a meal prepared by the congregation and gradually overcame the language barriers, learning a little about each other's lives. It takes some time for trust to build up. Towards the end of the meal, the teenaged girls shyly came up to me with a picture and an address. The family in the photograph were refugees from El Salvador, had been harboured illegally by the congregation for some months, and now were in Kitchener. Could I look them up to find out if they were all right and to say that their Mexican friends still thought about them?

This rich experience of Christian gathering in Mexico City has remained with me and brings fresh insights whenever I reflect upon it. It is for me a story of being included. I would not recommend the liturgy as a model to be followed, but the experience taken as a whole has a lot to teach us about inclusive worship.

First, there is the question of language. In this case not knowing the country's language raised barriers for the visitors to full participation in the act of worship. This barrier was partially overcome through the use of interpretation and the singing of familiar hymns, but the experience led me to reflect on how alienating our liturgies can be if they do not attempt to include with words the many and varied thoughts and feelings people wish to express before God, even when there is a common language.

In North America and Europe the debate over inclusive liturgical language began with the issue of including images that would be expressive of the experience of women into a vocabulary that is predominantly male. However, while this is still a concern, the debate has broadened to include the religious experiences of many other groups, such as children and aboriginal peoples. It is clear that the images we have for speaking of God's activity and of human religious experience cannot each be totally inclusive. The question before us now is the courage to use a variety of images, and it is perhaps more appropriate to speak of expansive than of inclusive language.

As an illustration of how language can be expansive, I remember giving a workshop on the subject of inclusive worship, and using a meditation in which the author employs powerful and concrete images of birth-giving to speak of the transforming work of the Holy Spirit. Afterwards people expressed their reactions, both positive and negative, to this arresting meditation. The reactions of two people stand out for me, probably because they were so unexpected. Two men spoke about how much they had been affected, and how the images had given them words to express the religious dimension of deeply felt experiences. One man was an obstetrician and the other a father who had participated in the birth of his child. To speak of the womb of God was not simply being inclusive of the experience of women, it was expanding the awareness of God's presence and activity in the great mystery that is present at every human birth. (The term *womb-love* is used by Hosea to speak of God's great love for Israel.)

Fortunately there are now many good resources to help congregations expand the vocabulary they use to express their deepest prayers to God. We only need the courage to try, the conviction that the effort is worthwhile, the permission to experiment, and the humility to submit our efforts to the evaluation of the larger church. I am reminded that the little Spanish-speaking Mennonite congregation cared enough about inclusive language to ask each of us to speak of our faith in our own tongues.

Second, closely tied to the issue of language in liturgy is that of culture and race. T.S. Eliot remarked that at times he had intimations that culture was the incarnation of the religion of a people. One of the implications of this remark is that culture is in a symbiotic relationship with religion: each affects the other. We are now familiar with the variety of specifically Christian experiences from around the world and the corresponding variety of theologies these have produced. In addition to the North American and European theology, there are now well-developed theologies from parts of North America, Latin America, Africa, and Asia with very different emphases from their parents. In North America the re-emergence of native spirituality and its encounter with European-based Christianity is providing both challenge and learning for native and non-native Christians.

The relations between culture and religion and the challenge presented by the resulting diversity to our understanding of God is perhaps the most pressing theological question confronting Christians today. A young Korean theologian made a presentation to the World Council of Churches assembly in Canberra on the subject of the Holy Spirit in which she used drums, costumes, and dances normally associated with the spirit life of traditional Korean religion. This presentation shocked some and delighted others. The same question is very much present in North America as aboriginal peoples recover their traditional spirituality and then wrestle with the relations this spirituality has with the European-based Christianity they learned from the white man.

The congregation in Mexico did their best to include for one day representatives from other cultures, welcoming even people they regarded as coming from oppressive cultures. In the course of the day they had at least a glimmer of the wider church from us, and were, we hope, enriched by the experience. Our congregations do not need to wait for the visit of a group of foreign Christians to experience cultural and religious diversity. That possibility is already a reality in nearly every community in Canada and the U.S.A. The pressing theological question is present for every congregation in a very practical way. It is not only a question of making welcoming space in our liturgies for a new cultural and religious diversity, it is finding ways that this diversity may enrich and expand our vision of God.

The third insight I received from my Mexican hosts about inclusive worship had to do with money. They were urban peasants. A typical salary would have been a miniscule fraction of mine. Yet they were my hosts and had prepared a meal for me to eat. In that situation the only thing to do was to accept with graciousness and gratitude the hospitality that was offered. It would have been ungracious to comment on their poverty, to say how much this must have cost them, to offer to pay.... Far better to say how much I enjoyed the meal, to enquire about their lives, to try a little Spanish, to join in the singing. As it turned out, the most important contribution I had to make was to bring greetings to a friend in Canada. Jean Vanier talks about the profound possibilities for creating communion and community around a meal. And, he advises, if you're stuck for something profound to say, you can always say, "Please pass the potatoes."

Creating inclusive communities who offer inclusive worship is not really about getting more people into an already stuffed room. It is about creating the possibilities for giving and receiving amongst diverse groups of people. People need the opportunity to give in order to experience in themselves the wonderful self-giving activity of God. When you give you are truly a creature made in the image of God. People also need the opportunity to receive in order to know the limitless and compassionate grace of God. Receiving a gift opens up for us the possibility of humility and thankfulness. Sometimes we need a little discernment about when it is appropriate to give and when to receive. Also, it is a simple fact that in order to receive a gift we need to have our hands empty first.

How often do we create opportunities for people to give services which will build up the community? There is great concern for providing services for every imaginable group in society. Perhaps in the church we should concentrate on welcoming the contributions made by children, people with disabilities, the aged, immigrants, refugees, and many others, to our common life in Christ.

The fourth and final point I have had reinforced about inclusive communities is that they have an expansive capacity for justice. The Mennonites I visited in Mexico were fairly conservative in their politics and didn't seem to think too much about the social implications of their religious belief. Yet they offered sanctuary and support to refugees who were in their country illegally until they could escape to a country which would have them. Perhaps their own poverty made them more appreciative of the desperate condition of fellow human beings, and more ready to take in strangers. Whatever the reason, this particular community went beyond its boundaries to include outcasts and aliens at considerable political risk to its own safety. Somehow this little congregation had caught the meaning of the word, *oikumene,* "the whole inhabited earth," and they were being ecumenical by giving space to people who were being denied a place to inhabit.

Inclusive worship at its heart is an attempt to make our liturgies an image of God's kingdom. And we know from Jesus' teaching that God's kingdom, while inclusive of all who love God, has a special place for those who are marginalized and outcast by human society. A joyful picture drawn some years ago by a six-year-old girl says it well. The picture is entitled "The Great Feast" and has a wonderful collection of humanity gathered around a table laden with enticements only a six year old could imagine. But there is one empty chair. Why? Perhaps it tells us that our human gatherings always need to make space for people we have managed to exclude if they are to be reflective of the heavenly banquet.

—PM

Space

The reading for the Sunday liturgy was John's vision of the New Jerusalem descending from heaven. The children had been asked to paint a mural for the front of the altar which visualized that fabulous, glittering dream which closes the New Testament. But what was now taking shape on the paper stretched out on the floor was something we had not expected. Just as John had taken the actuality of Jerusalem as his symbol, so our painters and scribblers took Toronto for their vision. When they finished, their city had been transfigured. It glowed with colour and light. In the streets, men and women and children joined hands in fellowship, hunger and cold were gone. The air was clean, the lake was beautiful — even the Old Vienna dirigible was an image of joy! And above all, the rainbow of God's love overarched the place.

The mural was more than a delightful bit of creative exuberance: it was a symbol of the feeling of *place* which children bring to worship. Like John the Divine, they see no discontinuity between their world and the world of the Spirit. God comes easily to sit down among them. Their city can become the city of God. This idea has profound implications for our worship, for it speaks of the centrality of the incarnation in our approach. We have tended to flatten our worship for the sake of unity. The result is that our liturgies can be celebrated everywhere but are really at home nowhere. We need to re-examine not only the *how* and *what* but the *where* of liturgy. We need a three-dimensional celebration.

The first step in the three-dimensional liturgy is that we must take possession of our space. When faced with a large or unfamiliar space, children will often race around the place to discover its shape, its acoustics, its nooks and crannies. If they are going to play there, it must reflect their needs. Similarly, when dancers walk on to a new stage, they will always warm up and use the entire space, moving around the perimeters, feeling the width and breadth. They are all making the space their own. They know that their self-definition is reflected in the *where* of their play and of their art.

In the past, we have allowed the space to dictate the identity of the faith community. Our church buildings have tended to reinforce a hierarchical, exclusive model of the community: the clergy in a distant, unapproachable sanctuary, often divided from the people by physical barriers such as walls and rails, and surrounded by quasi-clerical choirs and servers. The congregation has been organized and immobilized in rows of pews. We have only to stand and watch worshippers arriving on Sunday morning to see the problems. People sit away from the front as if there is a radioactive field. Individuals seem almost pathologically unable to sit close to one another, spreading themselves across the space in small clusters. If our celebrations are to be characterized by a model of inclusivity and mutuality, we must look closely at the space we ask people to gather in. And if they cannot claim their space, all of our other liturgical arrangements will be compromised.

In communities where churches are being newly built or where a renewal of the worship space is possible, these questions need real reflection and discussion. Change in the church building is a *hot, hot* topic, and rightly so. The arrangement of space and furniture reflects the identity of the community. Collisions in opinion are generally not artistic disagreements. They usually indicate conflicting concepts of the faith community. Many experiments are being tried: circular seating, central altars, visible fonts. In most churches, however, the space is a traditional inheritance. We need then to consider ways in which we can help people create a new feeling of community as we gather for worship.

* * *

The liturgy was beginning differently that Sunday between All Saints' and Remembrance Day. On the altar was a mural of a dead tree, its roots reaching deep into the soil. As worshippers arrived, they were asked to go up to the front and choose pictures of people — saints living and dead — and paste them to the tree. Gradually the tree began to flower as everyone's hands pressed the wood of the altar. During this time, the music was quiet and reflective, a refrain being repeated over and over with ever-changing decoration by the instrumental and vocal soloists. The clergy took their seats with scarcely anyone noticing. The tree bloomed. The liturgy had begun.

Two things happened here. The common task of decorating the worship space and actually touching the sanctuary furniture allowed people to feel a tangible responsibility and connectedness with the liturgy — altar guilds have known about this great privilege for years! And the music gave everyone an access point whenever they arrived or however long it took them to feel integrated. The liturgy began that day with a non-exclusive, non-triumphalist atmosphere. It allowed the community to gather and define itself in three dimensions. And if we can feel at home in church, we will be ready to experience what the family has to say.

* * *

The narrator of the passion gospel on Palm Sunday was ready to begin the story of Jesus' trial and death. The congregation was restless, still shivering after a rather cold outdoor procession with palms. Leaflets were rustling. Eyes and ears were not ready to see and hear. The narrator asked everyone to sit and join hands for a moment. Chilly fingers were suddenly warmed up, and the physical closeness of a neighbour — perhaps even a stranger! — seemed to help people quieten and focus. As the narrator stepped to the lectern, all eyes followed her to the large, roughly hewn cross which stood beside her. As the story proceeded, people stood up in the congregation to read the dialogue of Jesus, Pilate, and the other characters. We never knew who would suddenly become a part of the story. As each event took place in the story, a child would come from the congregation with a tangible reminder: a pitcher of water, a crown of thorns, a pair of dice. Gradually, the narrator's cross was surrounded, her story illustrated by the simplest of objects.

Our liturgical space must also be concerned with the physical relationships between people, and between symbols and people. There is no point in asking a congregation to feel a common purpose unless they are physically connected, whether they are sitting in a circle or holding hands. We will never be able to shout the words of the mob at the crucifixion unless we feel that we are physically part of a crowd. Neither can we identify with the characters of the story unless they have literally come out of our midst. A symbol emerging from the community is a symbol which carries part of the community with it.

* * *

The prayers of the people were beginning. The leader stood holding a single lighted candle. She asked for everyone's particular intercession for the sick, for peace.... From all through the building, the petitions came, usually audible, sometimes whispered. And after each group of prayers, we sang a simple prayer of intercession, "Hear us Lord, have mercy on us." So simple that we didn't need the words or music in front of us. During each refrain, a child lit a candle and placed it in a large pottery bowl filled with sand. Soon the bowl was flickering with the flames of our intercessions.

Fire is a traditional symbol, and for good reason: we watch it with fascination because it is alive. The flame illuminates and unifies the space and the people in a dynamic, vital way. We are drawn physically to the flame because we know that it has warmth and life. The intercessions were not just some words which flew away. These were prayers which came from real people in a real place. And if they were there with us in a tangible, spatial way, then we could feel that God stood just beyond the light, listening and responding. When we pray, we need to stand up, open our eyes, and extend our hands to God. If the worshipper in the farthest corner can offer a prayer and see the light and feel the warmth of our liturgical hearth, then we have overcome the limitations of our space.

* * *

The planning group was frustrated with the offertory. Here was the most domestic part of our liturgy, the setting of the table, and everyone had their heads buried in hymn books and leaflets! When we should have been doing, we were reading. The music seemed to be taking over the action. The only solution was to get our hands involved with things. Instead of the usual elaborate song, we chose an instrumental piece with an easily memorized chorus. That got the paper out of people's hands. And then we made the whole family set the table. Everything was brought up through the church: the altar cloths, the candles, the cup, the bread, the water, the napkins, the "recipe" book. A stool had been placed in front of the altar so that even the smallest could get up to see and be seen. The action took time, time enough for everyone to become involved.

Again we were taking, defining, and dedicating a new space. We had been focussing on the lectern for the readings, homily, and prayers. And now we needed to move physically and devotionally to a new place, to a new focus. The table is such a strong symbol that we might feel that it needs no special attention. It always has the most beautiful place in our churches: its height, decoration, centrality, even its lighting all attest to its importance. But its very importance can hinder our community if the altar is perceived as a clerical possession. We need to find ways to assert its domestic function without losing the richness of its symbolism. Our worship should not be afraid of its own space. The truest respect for our space comes through our truest use. Whether we come up to the altar or surround it in a circle as a family, we must feel that it is part of our personal furniture, our personal space.

And finally, we have to know how to get out of our space. If communities hope they have an open-door policy which encourages people to come in and worship, the door should be equally open to taking the message of the liturgy out into the world. If, in the marking and dancing of our sacred space, we forget that the whole world is our home, we have failed. The circle can never be closed if we take the dismissal seriously:

"Go out into the world, rejoicing in the power of the Spirit!"

In a sense, we have to realize that our space is transient: it is not the church itself. We create our liturgical space afresh each time. That may be in a historic church building or in a school gym, it may be in an inner-city apartment or on the dock of a summer cottage. Fire, bombs, disuse, and decay may take away our buildings, but the heavenly Jerusalem comes, new and glittering, wherever God and his people join hands and stand together in love.

— DC

Tradition

A famous bishop of the early church was walking along the beach of his North African diocese. Ahead he saw a group of children playing in the sand. As he came closer, he suddenly realized that they were playing church, imitating the blessing of the bread and cup, and passing their snack around like communion. The bishop became angry, convinced that the children were mocking the service. However, as he came towards them, he saw that they didn't even see him coming: they were completely caught up in their little play eucharist. As he stood there, the sandy wind blowing across the beach, he saw that the children were carrying out Christ's commands with more reverence than he and most adults could demonstrate. The bishop quietly left the children alone. He had seen the faith of the church passed on to the next generation, and he blessed God for the privilege.

In a sense, we could say that the bishop encountered the authentic tradition of the church that day: the spirit of faith and renewal which the church passes on from one generation to another. Most of us will not have the bishop's grace-giving experience. We will have to agonize over whether we are adequate to discern and receive the tradition of faith and whether we are adequate to renew it and pass it along to our children and those in our world who have never known Christ. It is no accident that one of the most popular contemporary books on Christian spiritual formation is John Westerhoff's *Will Our Children Have Faith?* The title says everything about the dilemma which faces the modern Christian.

What then is this thing called *tradition* in the church?

The word *traditional* is practically a dirty word these days. It has all but become a synonym for *reactionary ... conservative ... non-progressive.* In speaking of the liturgy, *traditional* has become a rallying-cry for those who see change as a threat, and an epithet of contempt by those who want radical change. Even worse, *traditional* has been trivialized by secular society. A *traditional* Christmas usually means music and customs which were invented less than 50 years ago by profit-minded merchants.

The clash between traditional and modern in liturgical renewal has been a source of great tension in all the churches. It certainly underlies much of the experimentation described in this book. No faith community can experience change without tension and some conflict. What we need to do is develop ways to turn the tension into a creative and supportive environment where change and reformation can occur. In order to do that we should point out that tradition has two aspects: the first is the history and experience of the *local* community; the second is the experience of the *wider* church, the universal church. The local church carries strong and very specific memories which help to define the community. For many members, this *is* tradition, the way things have always been done. The wider church is open to an increasingly wider spectrum of thought and experience which extends far beyond the particular place and culture which defines the local community.

Different churches will have different preconceptions about their traditions. Many Roman Catholics will see a tradition of unity in the world-wide uniformity of their liturgy: they will need to rethink their concept of unity when they encounter the rich traditions of the Eastern churches who share the same unity but express it in very different liturgies. Many Protestants have defined tradition in terms of fidelity to explicit biblical precepts: they will need to expand their idea of faithfulness when they reflect that the observance of Sunday is nowhere commanded by scripture but is clearly an apostolic tradition. We need to develop a fresh perspective for tradition, to develop a sense of discernment about the past, so that we can grasp the authentic without being overwhelmed by customs which were valuable in their time but which have lost their strength. The following examples may help to illustrate some of the directions which might allow us greater understanding of tradition in the church.

* * *

The planning group was brainstorming about ways in which an upcoming baptism could be made more celebratory and more engaging for the congregation. The suggestions were wide-ranging: balloons, banners — the list was long and often eccentric. However, none of the proposals got at the nagging sense of dissatisfaction with the baptismal rite. When we addressed that problem, we discovered that we felt that the liturgical action was too small, too private for the people to feel involved. So instead of searching for new symbols, we decided to take the things used in baptism and make them bigger, big enough so that the whole congregation had to help. Instead of one pitcher of water, we had six jugs, some of them clear glass so that we could actually see the water sloshing around. The oil of chrism used to make the sign of the cross was augmented by a whole cruet of rich olive oil. Candles, white baptismal robes.... In short, we forced the liturgy to use larger, more generous gestures.

The result was dramatic; the sense of involvement was palpable. And yet nothing new or radical had been done. What had happened was that the power of the traditional symbols had been revealed when they were taken seriously and restored to their original fullness. In fact, several people commented that immersion was the next logical step. Baptism is a bath, just as the eucharist is a meal. Now that may be a *new* way of looking at the sacraments for many, but it is not untraditional.

A similar problem arose at one liturgy when the prescribed readings seemed to present a harsh and unflattering face of the household of faith. The Old Testament chroniclers were in a bloodthirsty mood. St. Paul was feeling a little testy about errant Christians. And Jesus was very annoyed at the quarrelling disciples. The planners were uneasy about all the readings. The simplest thing would have been to close up the bible and think of a more pleasant, more edifying theme to impose on the Sunday liturgy. But we chose to wrestle with these readings because the wider church has said that these passages are worth reading. Our solutions that day revolved around the issues of anger and forgiveness in a loving community. The young people responded to the themes frankly and sympathetically. In the end, the tough messages which all the scriptural writers were sending out gave us an opportunity to talk about the fragility of human community in the Christian church.

Again we could say that the custom of reading through complete scriptural books over a season in the liturgy had been upheld, and that the traditional pattern of the lectionary had proved a challenge and a blessing. In both of the above situations, it would have been much easier to dodge the problems and invent a solution which was superficially more attractive. Here tradition was fruitful.

Our task then seems to be a constant testing of what tradition is in both the local and the wider church. One of our tools has to be a close knowledge of what our parishes and congregations mean by tradition. In some cases, we will see that tradition is pure nostalgia. Thus, many may look back to the full Sunday schools of the 1950s or the popular youth groups of the 1940s and say, *there* are the traditional models we should be working towards — leave the liturgy for the adults. Here we must recognize that the local tradition was the product of a particular set of social parameters which simply don't exist anymore. The decline in attendance at Sunday evening service is probably in inverse proportion to the rise in the number of television sets!

Those attitudes about the place of young people in the liturgy may be part of a strong traditional pattern which seems to be breaking down. In Anglican parishes, we will still see the remnants of the following schedule: private infant baptism, followed by 10 years of Sunday school and youth groups, followed by confirmation classes, and then finally admission to communicant status after confirmation by the bishop. All kinds of factors have threatened this pattern. The Sunday schools are no longer "manned" by women who can remain in the home; the teenagers have so much mobility that they have no need of the church as a social outlet.

In all of these cases, we will see that the wider church has tried to address these crumbling customs with some fresh perspectives. Thus, the early admission of children to communion (an ancient tradition) has revitalized many communities. Similarly, recognition that teaching cannot stop when Christians are teenagers has changed much thinking about Christian education. Curricula such as *The Whole People of God* now presume that everyone — children, teens, and adults included — will be involved in lifelong educational programs, a much more traditional pattern of Christian formation.

On the other hand, we should also try to discern when an activity of the parish or congregation has remained a prophetic tradition in the faith community. In our downtown parish, we lost most of our geographical members to the suburbs in the late 1950s. The number of children dwindled and for many years there has been a general throwing-up of hands about the problem. However, over all those decades, a fiercely faithful series of individuals has maintained some kind of ministry to children. It was often disorganized and inefficient, but it was always motivated by love for the next generation of the church. Now the demographics have shifted again, and the potential for young parishioners from the neighbourhood is very real. However, the parish might have forgotten about its children if those people had not kept faith. Now the parish sees a growing mission to its own geographical district. We're still groping for ways and means to meet the challenges, but we must be grateful to the members who were real prophets.

Another example from our own experience involves music in the liturgy. Our parish has a long and distinguished choral tradition begun by the great Canadian composer, Healey Willan. His creativity and hard work still animates our love of music and commitment to its essential place in the liturgy. That love penetrated the contemporary liturgies from the beginning. It was simply inconceivable to celebrate the liturgy without music. And so there has always been song at the children's liturgy. The contemporary and popular styles are perhaps a bit wilder than Dr. Willan would have approved of, but he certainly would have recognized a tradition for which he lived: Christian worship is impossible without music.

Every faith community will find these authentic traditions if it looks honestly and critically at its history and customs. Sometimes the traditions will be healthy and flourishing; sometimes they will be a seemingly dead root. Part of the maturation of our thinking about the liturgy and planning for change must be a real spirit of discernment about the community in which we find ourselves.

In equal fashion, we need to look to the wider church and beyond our own denominational boundaries, indeed beyond our cultural boundaries, to find creative insights into tradition. We should resist the temptation to assume that change is just being imposed from "on high." In most cases, the enthusiasm for liturgical change comes from the excitement and sense of homecoming which Christians feel when they encounter a new expression of the faith which allows them to grow in new ways. For many the renewal or cursillo movements have opened up a whole spiritual dimension which they hardly thought existed. Others have been enriched by the beauty and passion of the Orthodox liturgy. Still others have found that modern biblical criticism has given them fresh, new ways of responding to scripture. These experiences of the wider church are crucial for our local communities for they open for us great potentialities.

A couple of personal experiences on the journey....

During a year in France, my family attended a Catholic parish where lay participation and energy were white-hot. At the core of their activity was a quite extraordinary liturgical commitment. They gathered for sung worship every day of the year at the same time in the same place. They had shut down the organ, thrown out all their old music, and used no instruments other than their voices. The project was radical and challenging, and yet somehow profoundly traditional in its commitment to the singing of the psalms and the reading of scripture. On wet winter evenings, the numbers could fall perilously close to the "two or three gathered"; on other days, the church could be filled with hundreds of worshippers. The music was shapely and singable — hardly great — but it allowed everyone to participate regardless of their musical ability. The sense of inclusivity drew us in and the sense of faithfulness sustained us. That was a new tradition within the embrace of an old tradition.

On the same trip, we revisited the ecumenical community at Taizé, now world famous as a place of prayer and dialogue among Christians. Much has been written about this extraordinary community, but one aspect speaks to our present concern for bringing the wider church into the local community. Taizé's priority is prayer, and it is a liberating experience to enter into their common prayer without having to worry if the parish hall is unlocked or the coffee urn is on. The silences are profound, the music speaks to the deepest emotions, and the message is simple: we are all brothers and sisters in the love of God. But as you end your time at Taizé, you are always struck by a feeling that you can't wait to get back to your own community. The joy of the visit is that you never want to stay: you are refreshed and then sent back on your journey. Here the wider church is saying, "Go home and offer the fruits of this experience to the tradition of your local community."

These are new but, I think, authentic manifestations of tradition. It is tradition which does not constrain and inhibit but which liberates and empowers. Our liturgical planning should always respect the experience of both the local and wider church. We need to know where we have come from before we can change or move in new directions.

—DC

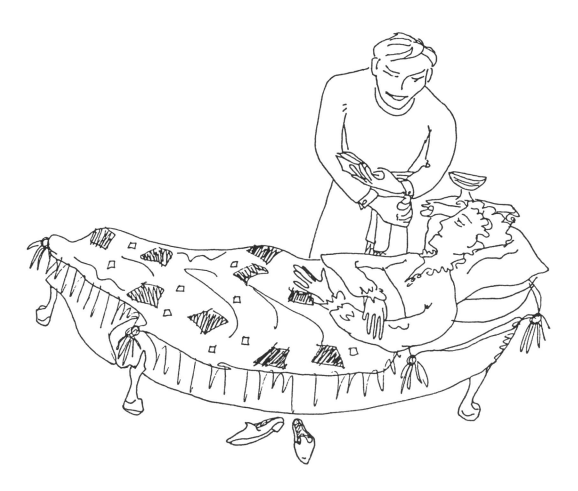

Politics

"I never could stand that man. He's not coming in." These words rang out of the
bedroom and down the corridor as I climbed the stairs, bringing communion to the
sick. That summer I was priest-in-charge in a downtown Toronto parish, and on
weekdays was visiting my way through the list of sick and housebound, none of
whom I had ever seen before. I forget how I gained unwelcome entry to this particular
bedroom, but once in I ascertained that "that man" was none other than my grandfather, an Anglican priest who died in 1931, that the bedridden but still feisty woman
before me had been a chorister in the church of which he was rector, that there had
been some dispute concerning the tempo of hymns and the speed of the choir's
procession, and that 48 years after my grandfather's demise and solely through the
powers of intuition which are often uncannily granted to the aged, the sick communicant on my list had correctly discerned my lineage and had furthermore with biblical
precedent remembered the sins of the father if not to the fourth then at least to the

third generation. This was not the most auspicious beginning to an act of prayer that has as one of its elements the sharing of bread and wine in a communal meal. However, I became so fascinated with her stories of church life in Toronto in the early part of this century, delivered with the passion of someone for whom the passage of time has become meaningless, and she was so delighted to fight her liturgical battles once more with a direct descendant of the original enemy, that we were soon friends and celebrated the eucharist in a state of truce. I should add that I had the wit to ask for and use her personal prayer book, knowing that it would be that of 1918 and that the liturgical innovations of the prayer book of 1962 would be unacceptable in this setting even though by this time "1962" was regarded in most quarters as "the old book."

In case I ever doubted it, this little incident forcibly reminded me that prayer, especially common prayer, is inescapably political. (*Political* is used in the broad sense of the word, meaning the arrangements by which human beings exercise power and shape their common life in a society.) I could see my ancestor involved in questions of authority, human dynamics, and the role of tradition, and I was the brief inheritor of their lack of resolution. These questions are with us today and are worth reflecting on as we seek to revitalize our liturgies.

There are at least two aspects to the political dimensions of liturgy. Although they are inextricably mingled in real life, as in the story above, separating them does bring clarity to our minds and gives more options for initiating creative change. The two aspects are the relations between church and society, and the relations among members of a congregation.

A brief look at the prayer books approved for use by the Anglican churches will illustrate how much social forces affect the way we pray. This example may well be true for other churches in Canada and the United States which have their beginnings in European countries.

The Anglican Church of Canada has inherited from its mother church in England a distinctive attitude towards liturgical texts. Through an act of parliament the 1662 *Book of Common Prayer of the Church of England* is the only official book of worship for that church. Modern revisions have been placed in an alternative book of worship which is authorized for use, but does not replace the earlier book. One does not need to delve too far into the *BCP* of 1662 to find reflected a view of society and the place of the Christian religion within society which is a firm antidote to the civil and religious upheavals experienced in England from the time of the early Tudors through the commonwealth under Oliver Cromwell. "The punishment of wickedness and vice" and "the maintenance of true religion and virtue" had very particular cases in mind.

Two and a half centuries later the pressing social issues were no longer those of establishing and preserving a strict social order in a single country, but of addressing the appalling social inequalities both within Britain and in the massive empire she had created. Yet the church did not have the freedom to rewrite her prayers to take these new conditions into account. Social reformers within the Church of England were driven to publish prayer books with the approved 1662 text accompanied by a commentary inspired by Christian socialist ideals, so that worshippers could speak the words of another generation while thinking the thoughts relevant to their own time. A.C. Binyon's *Prayers for the City of God* is an example of such a book. It must be admitted that many within the Church of England were quite content both to speak the words and to think the thoughts of 1662.

Similarly, the Anglican Church of Canada inherited the liturgical texts of the mother church, yet struggled to find a voice that would authentically lift up in prayer the concerns of the society in which the church was placed. *The Book of Common Prayer* of 1962 represents a major coming to terms with Canadian society while remaining within the English tradition, and in that sense it has a political dimension. The Anglican Church of Canada found its own voice even as Canada was developing its distinctive national identity within the framework of the British commonwealth.

Another symbolic moment in this process of self-differentiation came in the summer of 1963 when Canadians hosted the first Anglican congress in which Anglican churches from around the world participated as more or less equal partners. Anglicans shared with other British-based protestant denominations a sense of church prosperity and optimism in the early 1960s. Even though they might not represent the full cultural mosaic of Canada (nor the 29 per cent of Canada's population who were of French descent!), they felt some confidence that they were national churches, developed from and nurtured by a British heritage which was the dominant factor in Canadian society as a whole. For Anglicans the prayer book of 1962 was and remains very much a symbol of this early 1960s attitude.

Three decades later Canadian society has changed dramatically with people of British descent comprising only 42 per cent of the population. The commonwealth still meets, but Britain was nearly excluded from its gatherings over her South African policy. Commonwealth countries are for Britain only a source of tourists; the economic and political action is with the European Community. Where does this leave Canadian churches with a strong British heritage, still praying weekly in the case of Anglicans for the health of the Queen and all the royal family? It is not a question that is easily answered.

There are many profound and vexing issues in Canadian society. Our constitutional arrangements are under great stress; aboriginal rights and land claims are at last being heard; the cultural makeup of our population is going through great change; economic disparities among regions and classes continue to grow; environmental concerns are leading to difficult choices which will affect the whole country; a perverted exercise of power has led to many forms of abuse of vulnerable and defenceless people such as children, women, and natives. The list could be extended. Each of these issues has political content in that each raises the question of how we live together in the society presently constituted as Canada. Furthermore, each issue has an influence on liturgy if the prayer of religious people who gather together seeks to have any social relevance. Most of these issues are not settled in our society, and so it is not surprising that they generate considerable anxiety when they are felt in a liturgical context.

For those responsible for liturgical planning the main lesson to be taken from reflecting on the question of the influence of society on liturgy is a heightened awareness of the political and social dimensions to our prayer. For example, there would be little agreement amongst Christians in Canada on whether or not it is appropriate to pray for Canadian unity in the midst of the constitutional debates. These are important issues because it is not just society that influences liturgy; it also works the other way: we believe that God cares not just about individuals, not just about gatherings of Christians, but about human society as well. It is important that our prayer engages the society in which we are placed, just as Christians are called to be an influence for good in their social context.

Liturgy is more than a vehicle for the expression of social concern; it creates that concern in worshippers. Who can hear the prophetic recalling of Jesus' ministry to the outcasts and sinners or the cry to reconcile all things in Christ and make them new without praying for those things to actually happen in our social setting? We pray that they may come to pass; we also know that we pray for the strength of the Holy Spirit that we may be the agents through which at least some of this change occurs. And yet there is still another dimension, which is the realization of our own powerlessness to make all the changes for which we pray. We live in this ambiguity: an increased desire for justice brings with it impatience at the slow pace by which humans, including ourselves, grudgingly proceed to God's kingdom. This seems to be one of the inescapable effects of the interplay between society and liturgy.

The second aspect to the political dimension of liturgy is concerned with the group dynamics of a congregation. Any communal act of worship to a certain extent is a political compromise on which the members of the worshipping group agree. What music is chosen, which forms of prayer are used, are movement and dance included, are children present, is the subject matter of the sermon acceptable ... all depend upon the tacit agreement of the congregation. Any change in the status quo will have to be negotiated and may rekindle previous debates.

Congregations are held together by the ability of their members to compromise. This ability is especially evident in the growing number of small Canadian churches which share ministry. These congregations are formed by the joining together of two or more congregations of differing denominations. A wide variety of arrangements is made, from a simple alternating of liturgies at one end of the spectrum, to the middle ground of including elements from all the traditions in a single liturgy, to the other end of creating a new ecumenical liturgy that does not consciously imitate any particular denominational tradition. All of these possibilities are obviously the result of debate and negotiation within the shared ministry congregation; the negotiation is further complicated by the need to achieve permission from the authorities of the sponsoring denominations.

Shared ministry congregations have necessity on their side for engaging in liturgical change and innovation. Most congregations do not have this advantage, or at least do not perceive the need for change even if the reality is that they are slowly atrophying by tenaciously rejecting any innovation. How can a congregation's leadership keep its worshipping life fresh without creating conflict and dissension that become destructive to the very life that is being offered to God in worship? This is a question of great importance for those who care about the health of the church. The question is present in other places as well.

There is a balance which needs to be achieved in any institution between creative response to the environment (change and innovation) and continuing identity (stability and tradition). The church is no exception. In our liturgies we need both to hear the ancient and abiding story of our salvation and to sing a new song unto the Lord for all the marvellous deeds in the present. Furthermore, the new song will be much more acceptable as an appropriate act of praise if some care is taken to connect it to the salvation story as experienced and expressed in the tradition of the congregation. Identity and tradition are essential ingredients of change. Without them change will lose its purpose.

Each congregation has a power structure that needs at least to acquiesce to innovation if not actively support it. Small family-sized congregations of 50 or fewer adults worshipping on a given Sunday operate as a single cell with a few lay leaders who hold the real power. Clergy in these settings operate more as chaplains, fulfilling unspoken but nonetheless clearly designated functions. Any bright ideas that clergy may have for liturgical change will have to be carefully vetted by the matriarchs and patriarchs who decide what will fly and what won't.

The majority of North American congregations of all denominations are of a pastoral size, that is 50–150 adults on a given Sunday. Here the clergy have more influence, partly because they are likely to be fully employed by such a congregation, and partly because they are expected to relate to each member pastorally and become the conduit for most of the activity and decisions of the parish. However, this type of congregation will have a number of cell groups, each with its own needs and expectations. While there maybe the outward impression of calm and agreeable harmony, the raising of a controversial issue will usually reveal some surprising divisions. Because this size of congregation defines itself pastorally — typical statements of self-definition are: "We are really just one big family. The minister is so good. She seems to have time for everyone." — divisions can be seen in personal terms, and thus become very threatening to the status quo of the parish's identity.

One piece of advice for managing conflict in this size of congregation is for the leadership to assist members to identify their own positions and the positions of their cell groups, as opposed to the more natural inclination to be critical of other parishioners' personalities. Then the task is to create opportunities where the differing opinions can be shared with respect, usually in small, controlled discussion groups.

It is always helpful for the clergy leader to state clearly where he or she stands on a particular issue, and at the same time to allow church members the freedom to come to their own conclusions. If decisions are to be taken, then everyone, especially the clergy, should know what is up for negotiation and what is not. Surprisingly, the influence of clearly defined clergy leadership is usually much greater in this pastorally sized congregation than in the family-sized one described earlier.

The dynamics of the next largest congregation, the program size with 150–300 adults participating in Sunday worship, tend to be less personal. The parish naturally organizes itself into groups that each develop a strong identity of their own — a choir, Sunday school, youth group, etc. Managing conflict on matters liturgical often means mediating the interests of the various groups affected. If, for example, 100 children are to join the main service of worship on a regular basis when the usual pattern had been to keep them in Sunday school, then some very careful planning and public relations need to be done with all the parish groups over an extended period of time. Smaller churches often have been able to address successfully the issue of young children receiving communion in a matter of weeks. My experience in a church of program size was that the process took 18 months. While it is still important for the clergy to state his or her position, the real work of leadership will be behind the scenes with parish committees and boards, using some to develop reasons, support, and strategies for change, persuading others that the changes being proposed are in fact for the better of the parish as a whole.

The corporation-sized church typically has well over 300 active adult members and represents a quantum leap from the program church in its complexity and diversity. The patriarchs and matriarchs are now the heads of governing boards and committees, and the pastor, who oversees a team of clergy, is typically an almost legendary figure through prominence and longevity. The main liturgies in such churches are awesome affairs characterized by high performance levels in preaching and music, and a very visible structure and authority. These churches may adapt to new circumstances but they do not undergo major change easily.

There are not a lot of churches of this pure type, although we still have the buildings of another era with seating capacities of two or three thousand. There does exist a hybrid form in which several liturgies are offered on Sunday or through the week. Perhaps 150 attend one service and 250 another. These churches have avoided the grand and exalted liturgy in favour of smaller gatherings which can be more responsive to the needs of the worshippers. However, these churches still exhibit some of the structure of the corporation in their extensive programs and the group life which forms around them.

Working in one such church for three years I sometimes felt that the human organization was so efficient and comprehensive that there wasn't any room for the operation of the Holy Spirit. However, this was in the midst of liturgical revisions in England, and so the congregation dutifully undertook to try all of the options on offer. After innumerable experiments and questionnaires soliciting opinion on every conceivable aspect of worship, debates were held and votes taken at very serious parliamentary-style meetings. Change happened, but only because the congregation accepted a democratic process and the leadership played by clearly identified rules.

Churches organized according to corporation-style structures can remain healthy in a relatively stable society. North America is experiencing massive social change on a number of fronts, and these churches have been hard pressed to maintain their membership and ministry. One possible exception is the Korean import of the megachurch which seems to thrive on social dislocation. One of the appeals of this style of church, which is patterned more after the movie theatre, is the initial anonymity afforded the worshipper; it is able to attract unchurched people, a group which the more traditional churches seem unable to reach.

It is all very well to give sweeping, generalized advice within the covers of a book. Managing conflict and change is never that simple. However, if we are to create an atmosphere in which the hearts and minds of people are lifted up to God in worship, then we have to take responsibility for managing the conflict which will inevitably come with change and innovation. Knowing the political dynamics of a congregation, which are at least partially determined by organizational size, can be a help in that task.

We shall end this section with three suggestions of a more practical nature for promoting change. All of these changes require that we become unstuck from a traditional pattern or way of thinking.

We have been held captive by thinking that worship occurs weekly and on a Sunday morning. Most congregations indeed organize a weekly service of worship at this time; it's just that most Canadians don't attend it. Reginald Bibby has charted the church-attending habits of Canadians over the decades and found that in a period of 40 years beginning just after the Second World War church attendance as a percentage of population has been halved. The latest research reveals that less than a quarter of the population attends a religious service on a weekly basis. These figures have been used to draw the popular conclusion that Canada is no longer a Christian country. Leaving aside the growth of world religions other than Christianity, which are subject to the same social forces that affect the church attendance of Canada's Christians, to say that Canada is not a Christian country is probably too strong and too hasty a conclusion. Other studies have shown that 60 to 70 per cent of Canadians attend worship monthly, and therefore show some practical allegiance to their religious institutions and seek from those institutions some organized way to worship and to grow in faith.

The implications for the local congregation are clear. We cannot change the church-attending habits of the population whatever we may think of the relative merits of weekly over monthly attendance. However, if we continue to think of worship as a weekly affair, then we will exclude nearly half the population. Of course we will continue to offer a weekly liturgy, but we should break out of the habit of thought that assumes this liturgy is normative for the majority of Christians. Instead we should look at planning some of our liturgies on a monthly basis, with the monthly worshippers in mind. These liturgies can be special events with attention given to significant times in both church and world calendars: the beginning of school in September, harvest, All Saints' Day, Remembrance Day, Advent, and so on. However, some care needs to be exercised in the choosing of dates, so that they do become real times of gathering. For some northern communities, for example, the rituals of curling season supersede those of the local church.

If we can think in terms of a monthly liturgy, then any changes we introduce at that time have a better chance of being accepted by the weekly congregation, because the "normal" worship is not threatened. I worked for a few years in an English parish where once a month all the youth organizations attended the 11:00 A.M. service, swelling the numbers from the usual 75 to as many as 600. Sober prayer book matins gave way to a more rollicking contemporary form. This would not have been acceptable fare on a weekly basis for the "regulars," but the weekly attenders were quite happy to accept the monthly regulars and the liturgical innovations.

In addition it should be said that to plan a good contemporary liturgy which gives expression to the religious aspirations of people at a particular time takes a lot of work. If one is using movement, art, music, symbols, artifacts, speech, and silence in innovative ways, then once a month will probably be a maximum for both planners and congregation. At the initial stages three or four such liturgies a year will be enough.

A further word of warning is based on the simple maxim that people plan their own liturgies. A person who is basically happy with the weekly pattern of worship will probably not be very helpful in planning a special monthly celebration. In fact, chances are they will block any innovations. It is much better to assemble a planning team from people who will form the new monthly congregation and protect them from the desire to veto which can always be counted on in congregational life.

The second mindset which needs to be challenged is thinking that liturgies are always the property of incorporated congregations or parishes. If we think that any liturgy must be done by a given, single congregation, then our options for change are severely limited. We need to become unstuck from our assumptions about where liturgies take place and who is involved in planning them. They do not necessarily belong to one congregation. A recent conversation with a lay person in Yorkshire, England, will illustrate this point.

In response to my enquiries about the health of the small congregations which were characteristic of the nearby villages, she replied that they had been revitalized by the introduction of monthly ecumenical services which were participated in by all denominations and which were largely planned by lay people with a special emphasis on including children. She couldn't speak for the others, but certainly the Church of England congregation was comprised of a small number of people all over the age of 60. By themselves they couldn't reach out and adapt their worship to include children, teenagers, and younger adults. However, in an ecumenical setting a new form of worship was possible, and this was welcomed by all age groups.

Similar stories could be told in North America where groups of congregations, either of one denomination or ecumenical in composition, have together offered a service of worship which included people who would not attend the weekly service of an individual church. Planners are freed from the restrictions of meeting the expectations of the well-defined weekly worshippers and can raise their sights to consider the worshipping needs of less frequent attenders or even so-called nominal Christians.

There is an additional benefit to going beyond the boundaries of a single congregation. Most of our congregations are small in size, and while this has the advantages of intimacy it has the drawbacks of constricting religious experience. There are experiences of worship, fellowship, and learning which are only possible in larger gatherings and which should be seen as a healthy supplement to the more intimate experience of a small congregation. If the larger gathering can be ecumenical, then the experience will be that much richer and will respond to the strong desire amongst most Christians for the churches to put aside their differences and pray, learn, and act together.

To think of liturgy beyond the boundaries of a single congregation allows us to include many people who are now excluded by the forms of worship we practice. Furthermore, the people for whom those weekly forms remain potent and meaningful should not be threatened by an innovative liturgy which happens occasionally and in another space. They may even find their lives enriched.

The third strategic area for thinking about change is that aspect of a congregation's life which can be called its *identity*. If a congregation is alive, like any organism it will exhibit both a continuing identity and a capacity to adapt to its environment. When the need to adapt or change becomes particularly acute, a congregation will often resist by emphasizing almost exclusively those things which make up its identity: traditions, history, symbols, and rituals. The message becomes: "Don't touch any of this!" How is it possible to restore a healthy balance between continuing identity and a capacity for change? Fortunately there is some strong biblical advice on this topic.

A consistent and dominant feature in the Gospel according to St. Matthew is an emphasis on the "little ones." Jesus continually warns his disciples, and by implication all Christian leaders, not to exclude these little ones because the kingdom of God belongs to them. By little ones Jesus clearly meant children; but he also extended the meaning to include other powerless or marginalized groups of people, and those of his followers who were counted as the "least." In other words, within the Christian tradition we have a corrective to our own congregational traditions. Whenever we exclude the little ones from our midst, we are not being true to the larger identity from which we take our strength and life, that is the teaching and life of Jesus.

By taking Jesus' words seriously we are given a wonderful, creative, and radical way of looking at our communities. Jesus was not suggesting that we cram one more category of person into an already overcrowded setting. Rather, he was challenging us to look at our communities as open spaces whose boundaries could expand to include everyone, especially those who can't normally get in.

Children and other powerless people in our society such as persons with handicaps, people who are illiterate, the unemployed or refugees, and persons recovering from incarceration or addictions, can often help congregations get unstuck from traditions which have ceased to bring life and only preserve the past. There is a strong biblical precedent for including the little ones in our worship, whoever they may be, and this precedent when used with sensitivity can be a powerful and acceptable agent for change. We have all seen adults who begin by accepting a new form of worship because it was planned "for the children," and then proceed to get more out of it than the traditional adult-oriented worship. Children give us permission to participate in and experience things we would never think of on our own. This is true of other groups as well. One of my responsibilities has been to be chaplain to a home for women with mental handicaps. They had a tremendous love of music which came through whenever they worshipped and in the occasional dances held by the home. They also showed their joy and affection quite spontaneously with unannounced hugs. In their company I learned a lot about worshipping and partying with fewer inhibitions. They gave me permission to enjoy life.

This chapter has been about the politics of worship. The political process is largely about how we share power, whom we include and exclude, and how we instigate and manage change so that all of God's people have their place in the action of worship. I am haunted by an encounter in a Toronto subway station. I was approached by a young man who asked if I was the minister of a church. I said yes. "I don't go to church," he said. "Would you like to go to church?" I asked. "Yes. But I don't like it there. I can't read."

—PM

Pastoral Care

"Look down, O Lord, from thy heavenly throne, illuminate the darkness of this night with thy celestial brightness, and from the sons of light banish the deeds of darkness." I prayed, with the great intensity and feeling that young, inexperienced curates are often prone to express. Later that evening with a busy day of religious activity behind us, my vicar remarked drily, "Not perhaps the most appropriate choice of collect for 500 visiting schoolgirls." So, after several degrees in English literature, I discovered in the early 1970s that I had a few things to learn about sensitivity to language.

We may, I hope, avoid gross errors, such as this clunker, in the 1990s. But have we thought through the positive ways in which our prayer, in word and action, expresses and is responsive to the lives of those who have gathered to worship?

The incident of the malapropian collect is not simply an issue of inclusive language. It reflects an inattention in the act of liturgical preparation to the religious experience of the congregation. Without denying the power of this particular prayer, is the image of God seated as a monarch on a remote and heavenly throne an appropriate metaphor for teenagers who are probably rejecting such thoughts of God and seeking for an experience of the divine which is more human, accessible, and full of personal challenge? Is it helpful for young adolescents of either sex to suggest dividing their lives into deeds of light and darkness when at their stage of moral development they are beginning to question accepted authority, seek more autonomous standards for behaviour, and find a degree of ambiguity in moral choices?

Liturgical preparation should take into account what people bring in with them to worship and what they will take out. In this sense liturgy has a dimension of pastoral care.

How do we pay attention to what people bring in?

"I heard sex mentioned more times in that one service than I have heard in all the services I've attended in the last 10 years." This was after a reading and a sermon on the rather sexy story of Ruth, sexy in the sense that the story contains all the great issues surrounding sex: infertility and death, faithfulness and compassion, affection and intercourse, money and public esteem, regeneration and family continuity. The surprise is not that sex entered this service so forcibly, but that, for this one parishioner at least, sex had been so absent in liturgy for the last decade. How could it be that something so central to human life and so present in the scriptures was given so little attention? If we have avoided the topic to this extent perhaps we have only ourselves to blame when we find Christian people and communities sharing the sexual dysfunctions of our society.

People bring in with them hot topics, damaging experiences, deep concerns for issues ranging from the personal to the international, experiences of joy and vitality. They come with a desire for healing and wholeness, for an opportunity to express joy and suffering, and for hearing good news that is directly applicable to their lives. What they bring and what they want can't be neatly packaged. It is dangerous and explosive. I believe that good liturgy attempts to acknowledge what people bring into it, and then gives these experiences and desires a shape and an opportunity for expression.

There are several reasons we don't do this well. We fear introducing hot topics in case we get burned, and getting burned is always a possibility. However, the point to remember is that we are acknowledging issues which are already present in the congregation, even if these issues carry with them great personal resistance. To take the example given earlier, the story of Ruth provides an opportunity to explore a healthy and creative sexuality. When this story is contrasted with sexual dysfunction and abuse, it will be liberating for some and uncomfortable for others. We cannot be intimidated by the highly charged reactions which are only to be expected when we raise issues which are vital to human life on this planet.

If the first reason is timidity, then the second reason for poor pastoral liturgy is aggressiveness. Who has not suffered through a harangue disguised as a sermon, or even worse as an intercession? Even if the topic is a concern that we share, we feel that we have been allowed only one way to think and pray about it and we lose any sense that our individuality is being respected. There is a difference between being made uncomfortable by the gospel and being uncomfortable because we have been denied the human capacity for freedom and choice.

Good liturgy is not aggressive. Having acknowledged the important things of human life, liturgy gives them shape and expression and this is done primarily through the use of symbol and story.

The central symbolic act of the eucharist comes in the four-fold action by which bread and wine are taken, blessed, broken, and shared. This symbol contains the story of the last supper, but also the whole redeeming work of God. By entering into this symbol we take on in our own lives the pattern of that work, acknowledging that God continues to take whatever of our lives is unconditionally given, to bless our lives for a particular purpose, to be with us in the breaking and suffering which always accompanies commitment, and finally to share new life with others.

In talking of the four actions as the shape given by the liturgy to what we bring into it, I do not mean to suggest that there is something automatic to God's activity, as if we were to start at one point and be guaranteed to end up with something called new life. Quite the contrary, God's actions are full of surprises and reversals. For myself, I have only been able to find any pattern or meaning to events in my life considerably after they have occurred. However, when we speak of the liturgy giving shape and expression to the important things of human life, we mean that those things are brought into contact with the story or symbol which the followers of Jesus tell as central to their lives. They might have said, "Jesus did these things at the last meal he shared with his friends. They were very significant, and helped to explain his whole attitude to life, why he accepted all sorts of people who were socially unacceptable. He brought blessing to their lives. To behave this way cost him his own life. There was an experience we call the resurrection, which simply has to be shared." It is an act of faith to put our own experiences up against this story, because in the midst of our deepest concerns we affirm that God's purposes are for good even if they cannot be fully understood.

How does this act of faith actually happen in the liturgy? There is no formula. There are only stories.

A child with no self-confidence is asked to prepare the eucharistic bread, and presents it with shining eyes at the altar.

A mother and daughter drop their conflict and accept each other's basic humanity as they exchange the peace.

A couple who have been painfully separated for some months are reconciled and as an act of thanksgiving together prepare and lead the prayers of the people.

If we are allowed to bring our hot topics and deepest concerns into the liturgy where they come into contact with the story of Jesus both told in the course of the liturgy and lived in the lives of those who gather to hear it, then what we may take out is a confidence that our lives are in the hands of God. I have noticed that there is much animated discussion after a liturgy which has truly engaged people and their concerns. What is often going on is sharing at a deeper level than we normally risk. We can only do this kind of sharing if we have some confidence not only in God, but also in the people sitting beside us who have heard and responded to the common stories of faith. We entrust our lives not just to God, but to other human beings. We take out of an engaging liturgy an experience of community.

—PM

Planning Process

The planning group for the eucharist was scratching its collective head. We had made an agreement that our children's liturgies would always take their direction and shape from the readings in the ecumenical lectionary. We wanted to avoid the temptation to choose only "cute" themes which we thought would catch the children's attention. We had been lucky and hit readings which moved us in new and interesting directions. But now the dreadful day had arrived: this week we had a difficult passage! The gospel was Mark's description of the Pharisees questioning Jesus about the resurrection of the dead. We were stymied after we read out the passage. What were we going to do with the story of the woman who married seven brothers who all successively died?

Finally, one of the planners pointed out that Jesus doesn't answer the question.

"Why?"

"Because it's a stupid question!"

At that point, we all laughed at the silliness of the question. Seven dead husbands, and then asking whose wife she was in heaven! Out of our chuckles came a realization that children ask the same impossible questions of authority figures all the time:

"If you could save only one of your children, which one would you choose?"

"If you ran out of water at a baptism, could you use tomato juice?"

In a real sense, we had found our way to an important insight into the teaching of Jesus, of his capacity to cut through polemic and custom to the heart of our relationship with God. On that Sunday, we focussed on the resurrection in each of us through our encounter with the God of the living. We had found that insight because we had looked at the episode through the perspective of children. And we had all grown in the process.

The planning for intentional, inclusive liturgy can be more than yet another endless series of committee meetings. It is an opportunity for real spiritual formation in the worshipping community. But we have to radically change our methods. The first thing we need to say is that the planning process is an act of worship in itself. That doesn't exclude the setting of goals and the assignment of tasks: the liturgy is always labour intensive. But planning which comes from a common, prayerful reflection on the demands of the gospel and the needs of the community is a rich and fruitful experience. In order to give that intention a context, we need to create a different kind of meeting atmosphere. Into our meeting we can introduce time for fellowship, for a meal, for sharing of personal histories, for listening to music, for reading aloud, for singing, for telling jokes, for silence. These are human experiences and from them come the love and creativity which can animate a community's worship. Let's abandon the model of the corporate committee room for the dining room of someone's house.

If we are going to have a domestic meeting place, why not a domestic membership? Worship committees tend to mirror the models of efficiency which we inherit from our business lives. And yet the "business" of the liturgy is notoriously unbusinesslike. In the eyes of the world, worship is a waste of time because its results are intangible. If our planning process is itself an act of worship, then our old models of top-down decision making are obsolete. Planners do not have to be there because they hold ex officio power in the community; they should be there because they are willing to dream and be creative, and they are willing to work hard to realize their dreams.

Whom do we choose? People with resources, people with mature faith, people with scepticism, people who can get their hands dirty. In short, a family of planners. And because families are inclusive, we should look for planners who bring a wide range of experience because of their age, gender, race, cultural, and family background. The most challenging aspect here is the inclusion of children and other marginalized persons in our planning. In many cases, this will involve a careful one-to-one dialogue with people whose whole perception of what is happening may come from a totally different perspective. Most rewarding would be a regular inclusion of children among the planners. In practice, their inclusion will probably begin with occasions such as baptisms and Christmas. But we are not being representative just out of a vague sense of democracy. St. Paul lays on us the obligation to seek out the charisms and gifts in our Christian communities. We should be looking everywhere for members who can commit to the growth model of planning. And we know that not all the "experts" in a community are ready or willing to take on a new, seemingly unprofessional model for liturgical planning. However, if leaders with authority choose not to be involved, there is a special obligation to keep consultation wide within the community. We must be ready then to challenge the old without losing the continuity of experience.

In practical terms, we look for a group of people whose interests and resources reflect the needs of the liturgy: drama, art, preaching, music, fellowship, movement. They should be willing to commit to a pattern of planning which takes in a whole church year. They need a creative flair, a tendency to speak before thinking, but having spoken be willing to think about it. They need to be playful people because the liturgy is in essence our mutual play as God's children. And finally, they need to know how things can get done. They should be able to plan the meal, do the shopping, the cooking, and the washing up!

"I wish we could have a service like this in our church! Could you come and put one on for us sometime?"

The liturgical grass is always greener on the other side. Many people despair that their own community's worship will never be as good as another church's. And an equal number are depressed when a service is imported and bombs spectacularly. It is confusing and demoralizing. But if we look closely we should see an explanation.

Why try to recreate the music of a royal wedding unless you have three million dollars to spend? Why plan Gregorian chant if the church's acoustics sound like a box of cotton? If our liturgies are to spring from the needs of our church community, then they need to spring from the resources of the particular community. And here we have to engineer a major shift of attitude. What you need you already have. You don't have to bring in the clowns.

The visitor who requested a travelling liturgical show was convinced that her parish could never begin to renew the liturgy. There were no resources and too much "anti" sentiment. A few questions were plied:

Would an inclusive liturgy be accepted initially at Christmas or at a baptism?

Does someone like to bake bread?

Do any teenaged friends play instruments in a school band?

Who acts or directs in the local theatre group?

Who paints, or sews, or sculpts?

Who writes poetry?

Who knows how to tell a story?

Who likes to talk on the telephone?

The questions continued, and suddenly the ideas were pouring out. For the first time, the visitor realized that there were resources that were there right under her nose. It would be time-consuming, and would require great sensitivity, but the community might be able to create its own liturgy.

If that possibility is to take practical shape, we must be intentional about a talent inventory in the parish. We could call it the Bushel Process — looking under the baskets to find the hidden lights. This can be done by survey, by parish meeting — but ultimately we have to discern gifts in unexpected places, and that work will almost always mean one-to-one conversation with people. It's hard work — the hardest part of the planning process — but when the planners finally meet they will know what the community has to offer and what can practically be asked. They can be creative because they are supported by a circle of talented, enthusiastic people.

But the planners should lay aside their telephone lists and calendars when they first meet. On one occasion, our planning group was meeting as the crisis in the Persian Gulf was heating up. Our conversation over pizza was full of anger and concern and fear. When we turned to the liturgy, we found that the threat of war kept intruding. We were gradually realizing that we couldn't plan without taking the shadow into our celebration. And so our experience in the world entered into our worship. It was unsettling. War erupted later that week, and when we arrived at church, the topic was in everyone's conversation. Our reflections had helped us take those concerns into the liturgy. People had been given a significant access point.

Similarly, we need to reflect on the rich tradition which the church gives us. The liturgical year provides a treasury of Christian experience which can challenge and renew a community. Perhaps our most valuable resource is the ecumenical lectionary which suggests readings over a three-year cycle. In it we experience the whole scriptural testimony to God's saving work in Jesus Christ. It is a challenge to take that pattern as the structural outline for our celebrations. Planning groups may first wish to read aloud the passages for the liturgy being planned, and then take turns reflecting personally on the images and actions and ideas which are important to them. The responses will cover a wide range, and sometimes the group will find itself going in a new and unexpected direction. Often preconceived ideas brought to the meeting will simply vanish as a new perspective emerges. From these reflections will invariably come a central symbol or cluster of symbols which seem to animate the celebration. Now the planners need to see and feel those symbols through all the media of art, music, movement, and drama.

One Sunday the readings were about widows: Elijah raising the widow's son, and Jesus noticing the widow giving her penny in the temple. As we reflected, unexpected emotions kept coming back: the widow's anger at Elijah and God for the loss of her son, the other widow's courage in giving a penny right in the face of the rich and powerful. The situation called for drama, and so the Old Testament reading was acted out, and the gospel was read dramatically among several readers. Before the first reading, the music created an expectant atmosphere. After the reading, a violinist led the people in a simple but moving performance of "Amazing Grace." Other songs emphasized the role of women in the history of salvation, and the eucharistic prayer which celebrates the Jewish matriarchs was used. The reflection on the readings gave us a human access point to the liturgy.

To realize these new perspectives requires time and experience, and the planners should be quite level-headed at this point about what is possible. On many occasions, wonderful ideas have been jettisoned for the simple reason that there was not enough time or the appropriate person was not available or willing. If the planners keep in close touch with their circle of talent, they will find the ideas emerging from the people who are committed to the liturgy.

Now bring out the telephone lists and calendars. Any event has to be broken down into time-limited, do-able tasks. The planners should discuss both who can do a task and who needs to do a task. The balancing is an important pastoral consideration which can inhibit or enhance the feeling among worshippers that they have real ownership of the liturgy. It will take time, but personal contact at the church and on the phone will be fruitful in building support in the community. At the same time, most parishioners are busy people. Their most precious gift to the church is their time, and planners must be sensitive to the demands placed on co-workers. One parishioner good-naturedly put her foot down when she was successively telephoned by three different planners in one week! Co-ordination and sensitivity are essential.

Some planning groups will wish to have a regular schedule for consultation and check-in. Collaborations among smaller groups are often particularly rewarding. The preacher working with a sculptor, a musician with a dramatist, a baker with a server — these encounters can create new variations and developments on the liturgy's basic themes. Working with someone new or unexpected will enhance communication and a growth of fellowship in the community. In practice, our liturgies require about 25– 30 workers out of a worshipping congregation of 75–100. That is not because there is so much work to do, but because there are so many people who need to work. The ideal would be a total involvement of all Sunday participants!

In the final consideration, no liturgy should be planned which is so complex that it can fall apart if one component goes wrong; be ready for illness and forgetfulness. Neither should the liturgy be so under-prepared that anxiety infects the celebration. The ideal is a liturgy into which people can readily enter and which is then animated from within. The active participation of everyone is the touchstone of good liturgy. And having planned, we should be prepared to accept what happens. We should offer our best and be prepared to accept our mistakes. Planners need to become participants. They should be able to give up control to the whole community and let the liturgy live.

In fact, the end of the planning process is laughter. We need to tell each other what we saw and experienced and learned at the liturgy. The smiles of delight at what went well and the chuckles of recognition at what went wrong will revitalize us and make us hungry for more. Every planning group should make evaluation an important part of their reflection. Analyzing what went wrong will be inevitable, but the most important part should be an attempt to see the liturgy as an encounter with God, not just a logistical test. It is important to talk to people after the liturgy and to bring their thoughts and impressions to the next meeting. If the planning process is an act of worship in itself, then the final evaluation becomes a telling of the liturgy's story, a story which becomes a new part of the tradition.

—DC

Rooting

Liturgical Shape & Variations

Experience in liturgical workshops has taught me that leaders of liturgy, both clergy and lay, have little common ground in their understanding of the basic elements of the eucharistic liturgy and how those elements are put together. This variation may be due in part to denominational differences, but I think it has more to do with local congregational traditions which have resisted the ecumenically based movement for liturgical reform. Clergy and lay leaders have often accepted these traditions uncritically or, where they have felt critical, have not successfully negotiated a change in practice with the congregation. The result is polyglot liturgy in practice and a lack of a coherent theoretical base for liturgical planning.

On the one hand local tradition is to be encouraged because it effectively expresses the spirituality of the people gathered at a particular time and place. On the other hand when the reason for local custom has passed into oblivion and the custom itself is of questionable benefit, the time has come to change. This is where a theoretical base, at least amongst liturgical planners, is important.

But when it comes to creating a blueprint for a liturgy, how much weight do we give to the "basic elements" and the "theoretical base?" Do we have room to manoeuvre? Can we create some variations on the theme?

The answers to these questions will vary according to denomination, each of which has its own standards regarding conformity and flexibility expected of the local congregation. What I propose to put forward here are the basic elements of the eucharistic liturgy as understood by a broad ecumenical consensus, and then to suggest some variations by which these elements can be brought to life. For some this framework may appear too rigid, and for others, too flexible. At least it will provide a common ground for understanding the liturgies that form the second half of this book. At best it will suggest a coherent pattern that allows for creative innovation to express the spiritual dimension in the lives of those who have gathered to worship.

* * *

The basic shape of the liturgy is comprised of five movements: the gathering of the people, the proclamation of the word of God, the response of the people, the celebration of the eucharist in four actions, and the sending out into the world. Each of these movements has a purpose or function which is reflected in the titles; however, we can't expect the purpose to be fulfilled simply by reciting the liturgical texts. We have to think of engaging the participants so that they enter fully into the movements.

Gathering

I recall an ancient member of our congregation, normally known for his conservative tendencies, remarking reflectively one Sunday morning around the time of the Chinese New Year that he would like to see a procession in our church which incorporated a Chinese dragon. This flight of liturgical fancy may have come mostly from a puckish sense of humour. However, it also contained a sound principle which is that before people can worship as a community they need some activity that collects them from their disparate individual lives into a group. What better way than for the entire congregation to parade around and through their church building under the glittering skin of a Chinese dragon?

Creative suggestions of this nature rarely find their ways into official denominational prayer books. However, they are necessary in order for each liturgical movement to come alive and achieve its purpose.

The gathering of the people really begins before any books are opened, that is when people enter the church building or congregate at some prearranged location. At its best the greeting that they receive is a simple welcome which respects each person's individuality and provides the necessary information and comfort for entering into worship. Many congregations ask a family to perform this function, so that children, youth, and adults are greeted by someone of their own age group.

The opening rite normally comprises a gathering action of praise or meditation, a greeting between the celebrant and the people, and an opening prayer known as the collect. In the Roman Catholic liturgy a penitential rite is included in the opening, and this is an option provided in other liturgies. In the Anglican Book of Alternative Services there are additional materials such as a collect for purity, the Kyrie, the Gloria, and the Trisagion. These are optional and should not be included one after the other in an unthinking fashion. The key question is whether or not people have been gathered by the time the collect has been said, always allowing for the fact that, as Joseph Gelineau remarks, the gathering of the people really takes place up to the offertory.

The opening rite should not only gather people into a worshipping group, it should also set the tone for what is to follow. If for example, the liturgy is intended to celebrate a major Christian festival or the beginning of the school year, then some form of vigorous beginning such as a procession which makes a joyful statement may be the most appropriate way to begin. Here are some suggestions for various ways in which to plan the gathering.

Processions are an excellent way to begin a liturgy. They are a brief experience of a potent biblical image, the pilgrimage people. In a procession people join in a common activity, moving from one place to another, and thereby do two things. They move from disparate individualism to sharing in a common direction with others; and for a short time they take possession of a space in which to worship. This second point should be emphasized, because many congregations have the mistaken impression that their church building is holy, whereas the reality is that people gathering and praying in a place is what makes it holy. When they physically move as a body to a place for the purpose of prayer, the congregation states that they are a holy people by virtue of God's presence amongst them, not because they happen to be in a place that others have designated holy.

This aspect of gathering can be further developed by having all the symbolic elements and artifacts carried by the congregation to the place of worship in procession. For the liturgy of the word these would include a bible, candles, and other altar decorations, and any other symbols that will be used or seen in the course of the liturgy. For baptisms, jugs of water, candles, oil, white clothes can all be carried in procession to the font. At the offertory, the gifts of bread and wine accompanied by containers (chalices, patens, baskets) and linens can be brought by a procession to the altar. These last two examples are of course not part of the gathering rite, but they do make the same point: it is the gathered people who provide the necessary materials to be offered in worship; they do not come to church to find these things miraculously there.

When planning processions one needs to think of who is going to process. In the foregoing there is an assumption that the whole congregation joins in the affair, and moves from one place, perhaps outside the church building, to another where the main part of the liturgy will take place. In large buildings with small congregations, processions of this nature can be managed indoors. However, these arrangements are not always possible, and there is the additional consideration that some members of the congregation may not wish to take part because of infirmity. Some of the same objectives can be achieved by designating two groups, one of which has gathered in the normal place of worship, while the other processes to meet them. In this case a dynamic can be set up through antiphonal singing, whereby those already in place greet the others who are coming to join them.

A variation on the processional theme is to begin the liturgy in one place and process to another. An activity such as creating an Advent Jesse tree or discussing with small children the various denizens of the Christmas creche can happen at the start of the liturgy, and may even be enlarged to replace the homily. Then with a joyful noise, perhaps the Gloria, the procession takes everyone into the liturgical space.

Processions are not the only way to achieve the gathering of the people. If the mood of the liturgy is meditative or waiting, such as in Lent or Advent, then it may be more appropriate for people to come into a quiet atmosphere and be still for 10 minutes. Quiet chant-like music can be played for either listening or singing. Slides or other visuals can be shown which assist participants to focus on the theme of the service. If this option is being pursued, then the clergy should be present from the beginning, engaging with everyone else in the corporate act of meditation, and should not make a bustling entrance to "start" the liturgy. (The liturgy began when people first arrived and started to pray.)

To summarize the gathering of the people: people enter and create a sacred space; they are welcomed with respect for their individuality; they are invited to enter into a communal experience; and they engage in an act of corporate prayer.

Proclamation of the Word of God

The basic purpose of this movement is two-fold: to listen attentively to the activity of God as recorded in the scriptures and to respond faithfully in a variety of ways. Most congregations are now following the ecumenical lectionary which provides three readings for each Sunday in a three-year cycle and a psalm portion which can be used between readings. The response includes a sermon or homily, the creed, intercessions, a confession and absolution, and the exchange of the peace. Some thought needs to be given to all these elements if they are to cohere and fulfil their purpose. Let us look first at the scriptural readings.

There is no substitute for reading that is done with clarity and understanding. There is only one way to achieve this, and that is to practice the reading beforehand under the same conditions in which it will be delivered on Sunday. While this practice requires some extra effort on the part of both the reader and a listener skilled in public speaking, the results more than repay the time involved. A practice session is also an opportunity for helping the reader understand the meaning of the passage he or she is reading, although any such help should be kept brief and to the point. The theory of four-fold authorship of the Hebrew scriptures is probably not essential for an effective reading of the first lesson, and overeager clergy should not take advantage of a captive reader.

Reading of the scriptures is a legitimate way of involving young people in the leadership of liturgy. Practice will bring self-confidence, so that public reading is a privilege and not an ordeal. There is no reason why adults who read shouldn't follow the same discipline of practice. The same standards of clarity and understanding apply to all ages. The one difference between children and adults sometimes is the ability to project the voice. If the combination of voice and acoustics means that the reading can't be heard, thought should be given to the purchase or rental of a sound system. Teenagers tend to be the experts in these matters and it makes sense to seek their advice.

Good reading isn't the only way in which the scriptures can command attention. Sometimes a passage will lend itself to a dramatic re-creation. This need not be a full-blown dramatic production, in fact a simple version using a few basic techniques from theatre is usually preferable. For example, the reader may become the speaker, so that the reading is delivered in the first person. The famous call of God to Isaiah can be done in this manner, accompanied by clouds of incense and preceded by a short introduction. The epistles of Paul can be delivered by Paul himself, seated at a writing desk. Some passages lend themselves to a dialogue, such as the conversation between Jesus and Nicodemus. In others an image or the tone will suggest a method of delivery. "My little children" in the epistles of John gave rise to the idea of a mother reading this particular lesson from a rocking chair.

A further technique which can be used with a minimal amount of preparation is story-telling. Here the reader does not become the speaker in the passage, but tells it as a story. A few sentences to set the stage and involve the listeners are usually in order. ("What do you think it's like to be blind? ... Well, let me tell you the story of Bartimaeus.") If this technique is being used, it is best to memorize the passage, without worrying about word for word accuracy.

Story-telling can also be adapted to involve children and any other willing members of the congregation as participants, although sometimes the characters need to be translated into modern terms. I can remember a particularly hilarious version of the wise and foolish virgins, who became bridesmaids and ushers with flashlights, some of which had dead batteries. The bride and bridegroom had to be given some advance instruction, but otherwise everything else was explained on the spot. The chapter "A Story to Tell" contains more detail on how these techniques may be implemented.

A steady diet of all these variations would defeat their purpose and put the method of proclamation ahead of what is proclaimed. But some variety to supplement well-read lessons is surely to be encouraged when the method chosen arises from the text itself and enhances the propensity for all ages to listen.

It is advisable to have music between the readings, and this should be chosen with both the theme of the readings and their tone in mind. Music which is sung by the congregation or listened to allows the act of listening to continue in another mode. A simple flute solo may be the most appropriate accompaniment to David's lament over the death of Jonathan, whereas we can follow the example of Benjamin Britten's successful linking of the story of Noah's ark with a rousing version of "For those in peril on the sea."

In many traditions the gospel is preceded by sung alleluias. The music is chosen to reflect the gospel which will follow it. In order to achieve a greater integration between the music and the reading, part of the music such as a chorus can be repeated after the announcement of the gospel and at its conclusion, thus putting the gospel in a context of joyful praise.

The homily or sermon completes the movement of proclamation, although in the act of listening, and in the engagement of the congregation in scripture and music a certain amount of response has already begun.

Response to the Word of God

Reciting one of the creeds normally occurs after the homily and is meant to be a response of faith to what has gone before. In my experience the theory is often better than the practice. Reciting the creed, particularly if it is the same one each Sunday, is not one of the most engaging parts of the liturgy. Choosing a modern creed from time to time, such as the one composed by the United Church of Canada or others found in the worship books of the World Council of Churches, can help revitalize this expression of faith.

Another way of bringing the credal statement closer to home is to frame it with questions and follow it with affirmations which are composed to reflect the theme of the day. A model for this can be found in the baptismal service in which the celebrant asks the congregation, "Do you believe in God the Father?" and they reply, "I believe in God...." The questions and responses continue with "Will you continue in the apostles' teaching and fellowship, in the breaking of bread, and in the prayers?" "I will, with God's help." Appropriate affirmations concerning respect for the environment, praying for world peace, practising reconciliation in human relationships, and many other gospel-oriented actions can likewise be inserted at the end of the traditional creed.

If the emphasis in reciting a creed is on the community sharing its faith, then this can be accomplished by dividing the creed into parts which are then spoken antiphonally by seating arrangement, gender, or some other division.

In the early church the statement of faith occurred in the eucharistic prayer and creeds were not normally recited in the liturgy, except at times of baptism. While there will be various opinions on the omission of the creed, even conservative churches would probably allow its occasional replacement by a suitable hymn.

The intercessions or prayers of the people normally follow the creed, although there may be times when they are omitted or moved to another place in the liturgy. The Lenten environmental liturgy printed in this book for example begins with an extended penitential litany, and so to have intercessions at this point would be super-fluous. (The same principle applies to the omission of a confession.) If these prayers are to be a response to the word of God proclaimed that day, then they have to be prepared with the readings in mind. Individuals or groups can be asked to prepare and lead the intercessions on behalf of the congregation, and they will be helped in their task if the planning team tells them the theme they have chosen for the liturgy

This is not the place to give instructions for preparing intercessions. What may be helpful is to encourage some imagination in the choice of intercessors. Young children may prepare an intercession jointly with a parent; other family combinations are also possible. The variety of ages gives each age present in the congregation a point of identification, and furthermore helps to develop an appreciation for each contribution that spans the age barriers. Similarly, intercessors can be chosen on the basis of their experience: an older person, a refugee, someone who has experienced God's grace in a time of crisis, a pregnant woman. Each person will bring a unique perspective to this act of prayer which can enrich the whole congregation.

Prayer is more than spoken words. People have to enter the act of prayer with their bodies as well as their minds. Several minutes of focussed silence (in which young children are perfectly capable of participating), responses sung to a Taizé refrain, lighting candles as each intercession is made, bringing forward symbolic objects, the burning of incense at locations throughout the congregation, all are ways in which we can physically express our intercessions. When used with sensitivity these physical expressions have the effect of creating a sacred space for prayer in our hearts and in the community which has gathered to pray.

If the intercessions include penitential petitions, then it is appropriate to omit the confession which follows in many liturgies. To include the confession with the inter-cessions has the advantage of allowing for specific sins to be mentioned that are connected to the theme of the day.

The final action in this movement of response to God's word is the exchange of the peace. Embraced by some and abhorred by others, this simple gesture has become the symbolic point around which approval and distaste for the new liturgies swirl. Liturgical planners may mitigate their damages or restrain an overly enthusiastic approach by clearly marking the peace as a sign of reconciliation which appropriately follows intercessory prayer and as a desire for forgiveness, particularly if forgiveness involves another member of the congregation.

How can the peace achieve the character of an act of reconciliation and a sign of God's reign? An introductory sentence calling to mind a special intention can be inserted in order to remind the congregation that they are not simply greeting their friends. On appropriate occasions a special group such as children, teenagers, women, or men, can initiate the passing of the peace. The activity surrounding the peace will come to an end, of course, when the offertory hymn is begun. In the Roman Catholic liturgy the peace occurs not at this point but just before receiving communion.

The Celebration of the Eucharist

This next movement is based on the four actions of Jesus in the feeding miracles and in the last supper: taking, blessing, breaking, and sharing. The action of taking includes an offertory procession in which gifts of bread, wine, money, and other offerings are brought forward, the taking of these gifts by the celebrant, and the saying of a short prayer. The act of blessing, a sort of extended grace, is the eucharistic prayer followed by the Lord's Prayer. Then the bread is broken, and this action is accompanied by one of a variety of sentences and possibly some music. Finally, the bread and the cup are shared.

How evident are these four actions in what we actually do? How well are they connected to each other so that they form a coherent whole? Do the congregation become participants in the action or do they remain observers? Transparency, coherence, and involvement are the planning principles on which this movement is based.

Regarding the gifts of bread and wine, there is simply no excuse for not using real bread baked by a member of the congregation, although prudence might suggest declining the offer of home-made wine. What we are really doing in the action of taking is setting the table in preparation for the meal, and so the unbroken loaf or loaves of bread, the flagon of wine, and the cup into which the wine will be poured are placed directly on the altar for all to see. The symbolism of one bread and one cup should be maintained visually, which means that this is not the time to bring out the vast array of church silverware. The bread and wine are gifts of the people and should be displayed prominently in the congregation prior to their being brought forward to the altar.

Although some would argue that the gifts should be brought forward in silence so that the congregation's attention is focussed on the action and not on a hymn book, the most common practice is to sing a hymn while money is being collected and bread and wine brought forward. There is a third alternative in which music is used to bind the various parts of this action together. An offertory hymn is sung while the money is collected, then during the procession of the gifts to the altar the musicians play variations on the hymn tune, and following the prayer over the gifts a final verse or chorus of the hymn is sung.

Needless to say this action is an excellent opportunity for enlisting the services of children and others who need physical involvement in order to be full participants.

From the perspective of the pews the second action, that of blessing, can take on the character of an extremely long and tedious grace. And yet, the eucharistic prayer is the heart of the matter, containing a summary of the story of our salvation.

To overcome the inevitable wandering of attention during this lengthy prayer, one church in England has borrowed from the Jewish Haggadah in which during the seder supper the youngest male asks his father a series of questions which elicit the story of the deliverance from Egypt. In the Christian eucharist the children are given questions to ask which lead into the various sections of the eucharistic prayer. It is the practice of some churches to have children at the altar for this and the other actions. In light of Jesus' comments about becoming like children in order to enter the kingdom, this practice seems entirely appropriate for a meal which is in some aspects a foretaste of God's reign.

Some eucharistic prayers provide responses throughout and these are a way of trying to achieve the same effect. These responses are enhanced when sung in a truly celebratory way, perhaps accompanied by rhythm instruments. With a little ingenuity repeated responses and adapted versions of the Sanctus can be set to the same music to give the prayer a musical unity. Some of the music published by Taizé can be used in this way.

The third action is the breaking of the bread and the pouring of wine into the required extra chalices. This should be treated as having symbolic importance, and therefore should be done deliberately and in full view of the people. All those who will serve communion can participate in this act of breaking. Suitable music can aid the atmosphere of meditation which accompanies this action. Then, when all the bread and wine are prepared, the people are invited to participate in the fourth action with the announcement, "The gifts of God for the people of God."

There are many ways of doing the fourth action, each with its own legitimacy. Small congregations are able to gather around the altar and perhaps each person serves his or her neighbour. In large gatherings several communion stations are set up and people approach one by one. Whatever method is chosen, we should not lose sight of the central meaning of this action, which is that we are sharing holy and life-giving food. This meaning was captured for me one Sunday when I observed one of the clergy on his knees serving communion with great dignity to a three year old.

Sending into the World

The shorter this last movement, the better. It should not be cluttered up with consuming the leftovers and cleaning the dishes. We sing a vigorous hymn, we say a final prayer of thanksgiving, we are sent into the world, and we go on our way rejoicing. A blessing is traditional in many churches, but not really necessary. If it is used, it can be combined with the dismissory sentence by following both with a sung refrain.

Conclusion

A commendable practice has developed in which announcements of all types are made at this point in the service by members of the congregation. Announcements can be a good test of the bridge between the eucharistic action and the continuing activity of Christians in the world. Do they suggest that people are involved in activities of community building, reconciliation, and liberation? Has the eucharist in fact had the effect of patterning people's lives?

Another litmus test for the effect of the eucharist is the conduct of the coffee hour. Does it in fact include juice, soft drinks, and doughnuts so that all tastes are catered for and people of all ages are made welcome? A time for conversation after the service is not universally desired, especially by children who generally have a horror of seeing their parents disappear into the church hall for interminable lengths of time. While coffee hours are often the one occasion during the week when friends have the opportunity to gather, they can also be very excluding to the unsuspecting newcomer who has been lured into the hall with promises of warmth and friendship. Here is the first practical challenge to live the eucharist we have just celebrated, that is to live for others and not ourselves.

—PM

To Everything There Is a Season

"I feel like a new person in spring!"

"My birthday is next week!"

"I hate this time of year. My dad died around now."

We riders on planet Earth are part of great cycles of time and season. The rising and setting of the sun, the waxing and waning of the moon, the colours and feel of the seasons. And more ... the school year, the fiscal year, vacations, birthdays, anniversaries. Our lives are marked by the rhythms of time. Without those rhythms our lives are diminished. Hostages kept in isolation have often reflected afterwards that the greatest indignity they suffered was the loss of time: unable to count their lives by the dawn of a new day or the budding of spring, they could not hope.

The human impulse to find meaning in the passage of time transcends all cultures and ages. We all feel the impulse to celebrate, to commemorate, to communicate. As Christians, we inherit a rich tradition which invites us to join our own lives with the pattern which we call the liturgical or church year.

"T.G.I.F. — Thank God it's Friday!"

Our first pattern is a familiar one: the week. Although we talk about the *weekend*, if we look at a calendar we will see that Sunday is still the first day of the week. The earliest Christians gathered on that day to remember the resurrection of Jesus on the first day of the week. And because we humans are forgetful sorts, the celebration of Sunday became the regular time when the family of God came together to refresh and strengthen itself with an encounter with the life-giving presence of the risen Lord. So ancient is this gathering that it predates the writing of the New Testament books. Having spoken of the history of Sunday, we should perhaps mention that Sunday was a regular working day for the early Christians. In our rushed-off-its-feet society, we need to remember that Sunday was not always a privileged day of rest: there was another time when we Christians had to juggle the stresses of work, home and church.

And yet the first day of the week was never forgotten. People struggled and worked and even died to meet Christ in the weekly gathering of the church. The weekly celebration of Sunday is a challenge. There is the comfort of the familiar, of the expected, but we must also look to the prophetic and the unknown. Sunday must surprise us, just as the women in the garden or the travellers on the road were surprised.

As the celebration of the resurrection stands at the head of our week, so too it stands at the centre of our year. We will return to Easter shortly, but through all the twists and turns of the church calendar, we should keep one principle in mind: the resurrection is the centre of our faith and the centre of our life together in celebration.

As an Easter people, we will always find ourselves anticipating and responding to the celebration of the resurrection. Our first signpost on the road to Easter is the Advent-Christmas-Epiphany season.

And what anticipation there is!

Even in times of recession, depression, or oppression, nothing can take away the exhilarating rush towards the celebration of the coming of Jesus into world. But those four December Sundays of Advent are more than anticipation of a charming story. The readings for the season seem to be all over the place: the call of John the Baptist, the second coming ... the shepherds and wise men seem strangely absent.

The key lies in that rush of anticipation. We are asked to long for justice and peace, for personal renewal and liberation, for light in the darkness. Christ will come in many ways; he will have many advents. The weeks before Christmas are a season of prophecy and reflection, of trumpets and silences, of death and growth. They should surprise us.

Christmas seems an easy celebration. Full churches with hefty collections, reunited families, vacation time, beautiful music, good will to all.... But come Boxing Day, it all gets thrown out with the Christmas tree. To many Christians, it seems that the celebration has been side-tracked with consumer self-indulgence. Perhaps we should take the admonitions of the Twelve Days of Christmas seriously. Just when the rest of the world is giving up the festival, we should be just beginning. The church asks us to celebrate those 12 days until Epiphany on January 6. On that day, we remember Jesus' revelation to the world through the visit of the magi. We grow up with Jesus during those days.

The 12 days of Christmastide are a time of poetry and mystery, a time when God speaks to us through story and symbol, through song and colour. It is our most sensual season. And our most mysterious. The Word becoming flesh seems all but incomprehensible. We need to recover the sense of joy in the unknown which is the real spirit of Christmas. That means opening our imaginations to the poetry of the narratives, and recognizing the limitless possibilities of God's love in our lives and our world.

"Am I supposed to feel sad during Lent?"

The five Sundays of Lent which lead up to Easter are easily the most misunderstood season of the church year. The popular conception of a gloomy time of self-flagellation has hidden the riches of a season of growth. A glance at the readings indicates more than ritual hand-wringing. We see the renewal of covenant, of forgiveness, of healing, of faith restored. Nothing gloomy here! We need to jettison some of the cliches about Lent. To answer the teenager's question above, we don't have to feel sad during Lent. But we do need to use some of the traditions more creatively: silence, reflection, mutual support, inquiry. These lead the faith community into a deeper awareness of its own potential for renewal. Lent is traditionally the preparation for Easter, a time when we both individually and collectively ready ourselves for the approaching drama.

And drama is the essence of Holy Week! At no other time of the year are we caught up with the story of Jesus of Nazareth more than in the headlong rush of events which sweeps across the pages of our readings and across the emotions of us participants. The entry into Jerusalem on Palm Sunday, the last supper on Maundy Thursday and the crucifixion on Good Friday.... We seem to touch a reality which is palpable. Even in a secular society, people still go to concerts and plays in large numbers at this time of the year. The need for drama, for catharsis, for a cleansing of the emotions is still there.

It starts with a candle being lit on Saturday evening.

Just as the child Jesus watched his mother bless the evening Sabbath lamp, so the church begins Easter with light. Soon the darkness is filled with the glow of candles, and we celebrate Christ's continuing victory over the night of sin and injustice. No matter where we are in our own lives, we can join all our hopes and fears to the warming, invigorating, beckoning light of Jesus Christ. We celebrate with all creation — yes, even with Easter bunnies — the new life to which we are called.

And there's more! The Easter season invites us to celebrate for 50 days until Pentecost. The readings are magnificent. The gospels recount Christ's resurrection ministry, while the New Testament readings from Acts chronicle the early Christians' often faltering steps to lead the new life. Finally, we reach Pentecost and celebrate the coming of the Holy Spirit and God's promise to renew and inspire the church.

The Christmas and Easter cycles are separated by a series of Sundays in January and February and in the summer and fall which celebrate more quietly Jesus' mission and teaching. During the three-year cycle of the ecumenical lectionary, we read through almost the entire bible!

In year A, the Old Testament readings from Genesis and Exodus recount the history of the covenant with Israel while the New Testament lections read through Paul's great letters to the Corinthians and the Romans. During this lectionary year, we are taken through the Gospel of Matthew.

In year B, we read the Gospel of Mark. The Old Testament selections are from the great history cycles in Samuel and Kings. The New Testament readings give us 2 Corinthians and Ephesians.

Year C is the year of the Gospel of Luke. To the Old Testament histories are added the writings of the Prophets, and we read through Paul's letters to the Colossians and Galatians.

This pattern of reading has opened up the riches of the bible even to churches which prided themselves on a strong scriptural tradition! Preachers have had to wrestle with texts they have never preached on, musicians have had to find music for new themes, and Sunday-school teachers have had to develop new curricula. And people in the pew have heard more of the bible than they have ever heard before in the history of the church!

"Only 363 more days until my birthday!"

Through this cycle of the church year are spread celebrations of the heroines and heroes of our faith:

Francis, the lover of creation on October 4

Mary Magdalene, the apostle to the apostles on July 22

Maximilien Kolbe, the martyr of Auschwitz on August 14

Marie de l'Incarnation, the educator in 17th-century Canada on April 30.

Some are familiar saints, familiar from stained-glass windows. Others are new and sometimes surprising. But like the birthdays of family members, they cannot be missed. The church is always celebrating the life and witness of all its saints. In this calendar of birthdays and deathdays, we find models for our own living of the gospel message.

"But what happens when a family member dies at Christmas, or I fall in love and can't even think about a bible story?"

In our celebration of time, we need to remember that we see, and feel, and remember time in different ways. We smile when a child asks in August if Christmas is tomorrow, or if a senior speaks of the funeral of a long-dead sister as if it was yesterday. We must have both those perspectives for our celebration of the church year. We need to feel the child's joy in the daily rising of the sun, and we need to feel the sorrow of the long past. When celebrated with sensitivity, the church year becomes both a comfort and a challenge to each of us in our personal cycles of time.

Does that mean we should include the observances of the secular calendar? Mother's Day, Thanksgiving, Remembrance Day, Valentine's Day? If we celebrate the Christian year as if we do not live in the world, the liturgical cycles become meaningless as real time experiences. There must always be a dialogue between the church year and the civil calendar. And yet the church year is a sign to the world that its priorities are not always God's. There is a tension which makes us question and wonder.

—DC

Celebrating

Advent & Christmas

Advent is the season which begins the Christian year. It is a time of waiting, expectancy, and pregnancy. God is creating secretly. A new world is being fashioned. We long for its coming, yet are fearful of its consequences.

An Advent Liturgy

We took the cue for this liturgy from the first reading for the first Sunday of Advent (year B). The final verse reads, "Yet, O Lord, you are our Father; we are the clay, and you are our potter; we are all the work of your hand" (Isaiah 64: 8). This speaks of human dependence upon a creative God who will fashion those who are willing into vessels for the divine purpose. On the other hand, there is earlier in this reading a great cry for God to act swiftly and come with justice. This same theme is present in the gospel where Jesus speaks of the coming of the Son of man with surprise and suddenness. We are to be ready at all times.

The planners picked up these themes in two ways. The urgency of God's coming would be expressed in vigorous music and in composing or choosing short prayers. Second, we invited a sculptor to lead us in an opening activity and to discuss her work as part of the homily. The opening activity reappeared as part of the gathering on Christmas Day.

As people entered the church they were invited to take a lump of clay and spend some time kneading, moulding, and shaping it. They were to make any shape they wanted. The sculptor simply helped people work with the clay to achieve their own designs. This activity took place around the font, which seemed appropriate because there was a lot of washing up to do. As the activity drew to a close the congregation began to sing, "Abba, Abba Father, you are the potter, we are the clay, the work of your hands" (North American Liturgy Resources).

The greeting was given, the collect prayed, and then the first lesson was read as everyone held their clay creations. Then the congregation processed to the altar placing the clay objects at its base. The artist had created an enormous pair of hands which covered the altar front and seemed to hold all the objects placed beneath it. The sculptor had displayed some of her work at the base of the altar as well.

Processional song: "We hold a treasure not made of gold, in earthen vessels, wealth untold, one treasure only, the Lord, the Christ, in earthen vessels." Verse 1: "Light will shine in the darkness, God will shine in our hearts with the light of the glory of Jesus the Lord." Verse 2: "He has chosen the lowly, who are small in this world, in his weakness is glory, in Jesus the Lord" (North American Liturgy Resources).

The song before the gospel was *"Maranatha"* ("Come quickly" in Aramaic) taken from Taizé.

The homily was a dialogue with the sculptor in which she talked about the creative process in very down-to-earth terms and passed some of her work through the congregation. The children had lots of questions for her. Connections were made with the ways in which God influences and shapes our lives, and how in turn we use our creativity to make or do good and beautiful things.

The mood of urgency was picked up in the intercessions as a powerful Taizé refrain was sung after each petition ("Hear us, Lord, hear us Lord, come, O quickly come!"). It was continued with Patrick Wedd's rollicking song, "When he comes, the Lord of might" at the offertory and several more Taizé refrains sung during the eucharistic prayer and at the time of communion. An Advent carol, "People look east," followed communion and then the powerful four-fold *"Maranatha"* was sung three times, in response to the concluding collect, in response to the blessing, and in response to the dismissal. This had the effect of reminding the congregation of the liturgy of the word.

The offer was made to fire any clay creations which could be parted with for a month. They were returned on Christmas Day to the church where they made an interesting addition to the creche scene. The children discovered their dinosaurs, snakes, cats, and other creations amidst the more traditional shepherds and animals. Without being too overt, the simple point was made that our creativity is a gift from God, and that we offer our creative gifts and capacities in God's service through Jesus, God's Son.

The experiential aspect of this liturgy was well received by all ages. Just the feeling of clay helped the meditation on that profound image of human dependence upon God more than any words could have managed. The music captured the alternating moods of dependence and urgency which mingle together in the season of Advent.

The Branch of Jesse

In year C the first reading, Jeremiah 33: 14–16, contains these words: "In those days and at that time I will cause a righteous Branch to spring up for David; and he shall execute justice and righteousness in the land." This prophecy of hope was given at a time of great crisis, defeat, and distress. When we think today of the coming of Christ, what are our experiences of despair and of hope?

On Saturday our artist worked with a group of children to create an old stump out of which was springing a new branch. This was done on a large sheet of paper (5' x 15'). A large collection of pictures from many sources was gathered together; they were images of either hope or despair in today's world. When people entered the church they were invited to choose two pictures, one illustrating despair, the other hope, and to glue the first on the stump and the second on the new branch. Gradually, an impressive collage emerged. The activity was drawn to a close and the paper was hoisted into an upright position.

The celebrant spoke briefly about the theme of the day and then invited people to speak about the images they had chosen. After a few further reflections on the meaning of despair and hope in our day, people were asked to keep silence, and then the collect was prayed. This opening activity and shared reflection formed the homily for the day.

Justice, Peace, and Integrity of Creation

In year A the first reading (Isaiah 2: 1–5) contains the remarkable prophecy that the tribal god of the Israelites will come to be recognized as the God of all the nations, and that the nations will cease to war through their knowledge of God's ways. This prophecy seemed to speak to our own times and crises, which have been summed up in the phrase, "justice, peace, and the integrity of creation."

People entered the church to a repetitive chant which was continued for about five minutes: "Wait for the Lord, his day is near. Wait for the Lord, be strong, take heart" (Taizé). The leaflet invited them to meditate on the theme: "We live in a time of crisis. A crisis of justice, a crisis of peace, a crisis of ecology. God is coming. God gives us the vision of a better world. Let us awake out of sleep and prepare for the coming of the kingdom." This theme was expressed in strong visual images which the artist had created as an altar frontal and which aided the opening meditation.

Apart from developing the theme in music, homily, and intercessions, some additions to the creed were written or taken from the baptismal service. The responsive Apostle's Creed was used, followed by these questions:

Will you strive to be a faithful steward of God's creation and encourage others to treat the world as a precious treasure with which humanity has been entrusted? I will with God's help.

Will you seek and serve Christ in all persons, loving your neighbour as yourself? I will....

Will you encourage trust among all people, by trusting others and striving to be worthy of trust? I will....

Will you strive for justice and peace among all people, and respect the dignity of every human being? I will....

May the living God, who has put these good wishes in your hearts, give you grace and courage to manifest them in your lives.

Pregnancy and Anticipation

The fourth Sunday of Advent focuses on the pregnancy of Mary and the anticipation of the birth of Jesus. Year A has the story of Joseph's dream, year B tells of the annunciation, and year C features the visit of Mary to her cousin Elizabeth. The planners wrestled long and hard with how to bring this theme of expectancy and anticipated joy to life, before opening their eyes to the immediate and obvious resource in the congregation.

The church has a statue of the virgin and child, and so people were asked to gather nearby. After the greeting, the celebrant introduced a pregnant member of the congregation. She spoke of the experience of pregnancy and what she and her husband were doing to prepare for the birth of their baby. The children asked questions and felt her tummy. What better introduction to the experience of Mary, and what better way to link her experience with ours on the Sunday before Christmas?

An Alternative Christmas Liturgy

In many parishes a great deal of effort is expended on cultic religion on Christmas Eve and Christmas Day. Two full choral eucharists with other services interspersed in a space of less than 24 hours leave everyone exhausted. There is a growing number of people for whom the liturgical Christmas extravaganza does not speak. These are children, young people, and adults who want a service which is simpler and shorter than the normal Christmas fare. They want an opportunity to express joy and thankfulness with some of the simplicity which seem characteristic of the first Christmas. This liturgy, therefore, is not complex and does not require a lot of preparation. It relies on the natural wonder and awe of young children for its spiritual power. The children, whose religious faculties have been aroused by the expectancy of the Christmas season, help draw others into a joyful celebration.

On Christmas morning the liturgy began at the creche. A recorder and a guitar led the gathering congregation in a selection of carols. Children had been invited to bring their present from Santa. The celebrant greeted the congregation, then asked the children to show their presents and to describe how they had felt when they woke up. (This usually produces enough homiletic material for a year.) Their attention was drawn to the creche scene, and they identified the figures and how they must have felt. We then sang a carol which spoke of the gifts brought to the Christ child by all the animals. ("Jesus our brother, strong and good, was humbly born in a stable rude; and the friendly beasts around him stood, Jesus our brother, strong and good.")

A prayer was said, and then the story was briefly and dramatically told of the surprising visit of the angels to the shepherds. We took up the candles and a cloth for the altar, the book in which the story of Jesus is contained, and our presents, and processed into the church singing the song of the angels to a Taizé refrain. When we arrived, the altar was dressed and presents were laid at its base for those who wished (with assurances that they would be returned), the collect for the day was prayed, and we began the liturgy of the word. There isn't much more to add by way of guidance to liturgical planners, except to say that simplicity, brevity, and joy characterized the choice of music, the homily, and intercessions, and all other parts of the liturgy, so that the tone set at the beginning of the service was carried throughout. It is particularly appropriate for children to take leadership roles, be engaged in the liturgy of the word, and be present at the altar during the eucharistic prayer. After the dismissal, a few festive cookies, a short social time, and then everyone scattered to the many and varied saturnalian observances with family and friends.

Baptismal Liturgy

The baptismal liturgy is the liturgy most in need of reform. There has been considerable theological work done on the meaning of baptism which has tried to restore this action to the centre of Christian life. Catechumenate programs have drawn from the experience of the fourth-century church to provide adults seeking baptism with training and instruction prior to the rite. In many places parents seeking baptism for their children are expected to attend classes of instruction and to become active members of the congregation if they are not already. However, all this pressure from the institutional church has not taken into account the role of baptism from the point of view of those who come seeking baptism in the first place. Furthermore, most baptismal liturgies remain pale and formalized rites which are paltry advertisements for the eternal life which is the animating theme of baptism.

Theological Renewal

In baptism it could be said that we join a large international corporation through a branch plant. Membership requires total dependence upon the Founder and engagement in various activities of service and mission. For the corporation the minimum requirement is usually attendance at the meetings, and a lot of effort has gone into convincing wary inquirers that there is in fact a logical link between the rite of baptism and joining the organization. For many people who explore baptism for themselves or their children, this request for participation may come as a novelty.

The real issue is making a connection between what the church says baptism is about and the intricate web of relationships which comprise people's lives. The biblical language and imagery associated with baptism are richly symbolic and have the potential for making these connections, although it should be said that the connections are not automatic and the symbols may not all have retained their original power over 20 centuries. At any rate, a brief theological summary of the meaning of baptism is that through baptism we share in the whole work of God's salvation in Christ: we participate in Christ's death and resurrection, and we receive the gift of the Spirit. There are a host of biblical images through which the church has sought in its baptismal liturgies to express the central mystery of salvation:

> participation in Christ's death and resurrection (Romans 6: 3–5)
> a new birth (John 3: 5)
> an enlightenment by Christ (Ephesians 5: 14)
> a reclothing in Christ (Galatians 3: 27)
> a renewal by the Spirit (Titus 3: 5)
> the experience of salvation from the flood (1 Peter 3: 20–21)
> an exodus from bondage (1 Corinthians 10: 1–2)
> a liberation into a new humanity (Galatians 3: 27–28; 1 Corinthians 12: 13)
> a washing away of sin (1 Corinthians 6: 11).

The liturgies of many churches have been revised to reflect the renewed understanding of baptism, incorporating these images at appropriate points in the text. In addition the liturgical texts are often accompanied by instructions or suggestions about incorporating visual symbols and actions to further enhance the rich meaning of baptism. One can find advice about water and immersion, the use of chrism and signing, and the presentation of lighted candles. But how do these symbols, both verbal and tactile, relate to the context from which people come?

Family Renewal

In the case of a baby, baptism is a significant event for the family system. It is a ritual by which the birth is acknowledged and the child accepted. The child joins a society in a formal way for the first time. This may not be immediately significant for the child, but it is for the rest of the family. Realignments occur and reconciliations may be achieved amongst adult family members, and their children as well. Baptismal preparation courses for parents should give equal time to these aspects. They are after all not so far removed from theology; they are really a theology of the extended family. Issues of belonging, dependence and interdependence, healing and redefinition of relationships, creating healthy people who can give themselves in causes of justice, peacemaking and care for the environment, all these issues are the expression in family life of what the church is saying in its theology.

How do we discover the family significance of a baptism? We can begin by ascertaining who wants this baptism and why, who supports it and who opposes it, what are the hopes, fears, and expectations being focussed in the baptism which have their sources in family relationships. Let us consider a typical example of baptism by force.

"I'm having that baby baptised!" said the angry grandmother who never approved of the marriage of her daughter in the first place. The pregnancy, which began seven months before the wedding, was the daughter's attempt to oppose her mother and force acceptance of her partner into the family system. The grandmother had not been a particularly active church member, so her insistence on baptism was somewhat surprising to the clergy. Surprising that is until the clergy realized that the grandmother was using the rite of baptism to reassert her control over her daughter, and that her operative theology in this case was punishment and retribution.

In this unpromising scenario there is however an opportunity for healthy action. Instead of trying to wring a commitment out of the daughter, the clergy could take the position that she has a choice whether or not to have her child baptised, and that the clergy will support her in her decision. In favour of baptism it could be pointed out that joining the church is joining another family which may provide opportunity for escaping maternal disapproval and for feeling totally positive about her child for the first time. These more positive approaches to baptism would have to have a basis in experience, both in the preparation process and in contact with members of the congregation. However, by saying yes to the baptism of her child, the daughter has the opportunity to take responsibility for her role in the larger family system, whereas up to this point her behaviour was mostly reactive. Furthermore, she has the opportunity to include her partner with dignity and respect, perhaps by having the baby's father read one of the lessons.

These family dynamics are not escaped when the baptised is an adult, although they take on a different shape. Even when baptism is a clear expression of an adult coming to faith, there will be considerable effects on the family relationships. Consider for example a man who decides to be baptised in his wife's Missionary Alliance church. The repercussions would be somewhat different if this same man began taking catechumenate classes on the recommendation of a female Roman Catholic friend from the office. Whatever way you look at it, baptism is a crisis, very often of major proportions, full of dangers and opportunities. If we pay more attention to the family of origin, then those who come for baptism may be ready to consider giving their loyalty to the family of the church.

Making the Connections

Preparation and planning for baptism involves both these families, and both may be resistant. "Another distracting, irrelevant baptism! We won't see them again," is a sentiment that is not foreign to congregations who have had their normal pattern of worship disrupted by sudden influxes of uncomfortable strangers with cameras.

Church programs for baptismal preparation now usually include representatives from the congregation so that the two families, the family of origin and the family of the church, are brought together in part before the rite. The relationship between the two families can be explored through the use of symbols. These symbols are probably best taken from the baptismal liturgy, although they could also include the readings for the day on which the baptism was to occur. What, for example, does the symbol of water have to say to the rebellious daughter who married against her mother's wishes? What experiences and feelings are summoned up when she thinks about water? Perhaps a fear of drowning or being smothered? The symbolic associations of water are expansive enough to encompass experiences both of fear and of joy, of death and of life, of helplessness and of responsibility. It is in the preparation process that the various associations can be explored, with attention being given to the experiences and values in the family of origin and the family of the church. The exploration of symbols, which is often done effectively through visual images or music, can be a way of entry into the life of both families. Those seeking baptism can find a way to express their hopes and fears, while the same symbols can be used to speak of the experience of the presence of God within the Christian community.

Liturgical Planning

The liturgical planning should obviously reflect the baptismal preparation process, making use of those symbols which were most meaningful to the participants. The dominant themes are those of joy and celebration, belonging, and movement from death to new life. In addition there are all the considerations which arise when hordes of visitors join the regulars. How does one family show hospitality to another?

The baptismal symbols in this liturgy — water, fire, oil, clothes, movements — are not miniatures to be handled with care only by designated people; they are large and generous and are meant to show that there is room for everyone in God's kingdom. They offer the means for participation; they also convey that the event is serious and celebratory at the same time, able to involve everyone at a variety of levels.

In addition to these traditional symbols we have used others to express the theme of the day. The reading of 1 Peter 2: 2–10 ("You are living stones") gave rise to the idea of creating a church building of stones made from boxes at the beginning of the service, to bring out for each person the aspect of belonging. On another occasion, using the same reading, everyone received a beach stone at the beginning of the service so that these could be placed later in a bowl. Water was poured over them, revealing their inherent colour, and appropriate homiletic points were made. To emphasize the celebratory nature of one baptism, a canopy was created in the mode of a Jewish wedding *chuppah*, covered with dolphins.

Increasingly children are being born of interfaith marriages where both partners wish to maintain their religious traditions. Although some denominations are quite bold in devising new services which will reflect both faiths, we have taken the approach that baptism is a Christian rite which nonetheless has the flexibility to acknowledge and honour the points of agreement and commonality between Christianity and the other faith. In a baptism where one parent was Hindu we incorporated a beautiful Hindu prayer, used the Hindu word *shanti* wherever *peace* occurred, burned Indian incense, and sprinkled the baby with rose petals after the baptism according to the Hindu naming ceremony. These details were explored with the parents beforehand, and had the effect of supporting their resolve to bring up their child in the knowledge and love of God expressed through both religions.

The readings and intercessory prayers provide opportunities for involving significant family members, especially children, although this should always be done with
care that the assignment doesn't produce great anxiety.

Finally, if the baptismal preparation has been done well, there will be no need for
explanation during the service. If it hasn't been done well, the liturgy is not the place
for attempted recovery. Clergy should avoid the temptation to explain at length the
meaning of the various symbols to a captive audience. The symbols will speak for
themselves if they are believed in and made evident. If not, more words will not
redeem them.

The Liturgy

GATHERING

Children and adults functioned as greeters and helped the visitors to find their way
through the unfamiliar surroundings. Leaflets were prepared with the service printed
in its entirety, with the visitors especially in mind. On entering the church, people
were invited to participate in the activity planned for that day — creating an altar
frontal, making a building of stones, decorating the baptismal canopy.

The singing of the Gloria as an entrance song provided a transition between the
activity and the greeting. A lively version was used in which cantors sang the verses
and the people responded with a simple refrain which could be picked up very
quickly.

The celebrant welcomed the congregation, introduced the theme by commenting
on what had been created by the joint activity of the congregation, and invited those
present to enter into an act of prayer by remaining silent. The collect was said.

PROCLAMATION OF THE WORD

Readers were drawn from members of the extended family. Music between the
readings was chosen for its reflection of the theme and its simplicity. Following the
gospel, the congregation was invited to sit down, and the children to come forward.

CELEBRATION OF BAPTISM

The celebrant spoke briefly to the children about what was going to happen next. In
one instance this was done by asking them to place their beach stones in a bowl and to

observe what changes occurred when water was poured over them. In the same way human beings take on life and colour when they enter the Christian life through the waters of baptism. When the activity was the creation of a building the emphasis was on the importance of each block of stone for the whole building. They were invited to find their stones in the building, and to discover that one stone was missing, that of little X who was about to be baptised. His stone would be added.

Various things are necessary for baptism. The children are invited to get these in turn as a brief sentence introduces each one: many large jugs of water; candles, including one unlit baptismal candle; a large jug of oil; towels; white garments; the baptismal canopy; and finally, the baby, and the baptismal party. All these assemble at the front of the church and prepare for the procession to the font.

A joyful procession of the whole congregation follows, accompanied by a variety of rhythm instruments. It is worth taking time and care with this aspect, because the procession is a physical way of expressing a significant movement in the family's life, in fact, in the lives of both the family of origin and the family of the church.

At the font the candidate for baptism is presented with the renunciations of evil and the affirmations of faith made by the parents and godparents in the case of young children and babies. The congregation has one statement of support to make. Following are the prayers for the candidate, and these can be led by people, children, or adults, who have an intimate and healthy interest in the child's development. A sung refrain to these prayers enhances participation and gives a reflective feeling.

The celebrant can sing the thanksgiving over the water using a simple recitation on one note if other variations prove too demanding. The people respond with a lively sung "Blessed be God!" after each section, set to music from Taizé. During the singing of these refrains children bring forward the pitchers of water and pour them into the font. While gallons of water may not be strictly necessary to perform a baptism, insignificant puddles lying invisible in the bottom of fonts are hardly expressive of all the mighty symbolic associations we bring to the element of water.

The baptismal covenant is recited by all in a question and response form. In many liturgies, such as *The Book of Alternative Services,* the Apostles' Creed is followed by further questions relating to Christian spirituality, repentance, evangelism, service, and justice. These questions provide an opportunity for adaptation to the particular circumstances of those coming to baptism. Variations on these questions could be composed during the baptismal preparation, keeping in mind that they must be general enough for the whole congregation to join in.

To make the baptismal actions public they must be visible to all. One way to make them participatory and celebratory is to add a sung refrain set to music from Taizé after each. This can be the same refrain used for the blessing of the water.

Blessed be God! Blessed be God! Blessed be God forever!
Blessed be God! Blessed be God! Alleluia, alleluia!

N, I baptise you in the name of the Father, and of the Son, and of the Holy Spirit!
(water)

Blessed be God....

I sign you with the sign of the cross, and mark you as Christ's own forever!
(oil)

Blessed be God....

Receive the light of Christ to show that you have passed from darkness to light!
(candle, lit from the paschal candle)

Blessed be God....

Put on these clothes to show that we are all one in Christ!
(clothing)

Blessed be God....

At this point the whole congregation can be splashed or sprinkled with water to remind them that because of their baptisms they are now standing as a community welcoming a new member.

The baptismal liturgy concludes with a prayer for the newly baptised, a welcome which may be sung, and the exchange of the peace. One variation which has been tried is to ask the baptised person to speak briefly about the meaning of baptism just before the exchange of the peace. Personal testimony in the midst of public worship is not the usual practice in mainline churches; but if the person, child or adult, is comfortable with the request, then this is an excellent opportunity to articulate an experience of faith. Needless to say, if this suggestion is followed, it should take the place of the homily.

The peace is an opportunity for everyone (depending on the number present) to greet the newly baptised, and to express with a simple gesture a genuine welcome into the community of the church. Even as the procession to the font is a dramatic movement symbolic of moving from one condition to another, so the offertory procession which follows the peace is a joyful movement towards the eucharistic celebration of new life. If all the elements needed for this celebration have been placed close to the font — bread, wine, chalice, candles, linens — they can be taken up at this point and carried to the altar, perhaps by members of the baptismal party.

Given that there are likely to be a number of visitors, if it is the practice of the church, an invitation for all baptised Christians to receive communion overcomes the hesitation that visitors often feel.

Because the baptismal rite adds some time to the normal proceedings, it is important to keep the remainder of the liturgy as brief as possible. This is at least one way of showing sensitivity to the visitors who probably share the North American tolerance level of one hour.

The coffee hour is another opportunity for redemption, usually much needed. In many cases the baptismal family will be rushing off to a party after the obligatory photos around the font. It may be possible to offer some light refreshments at the back of the church while the photos are being taken and the certificates signed. In other cases, where the church connection is strong and friendships are present with members of the congregation, the party may take place in the church hall itself. A special effort could be made to have the refreshments appeal to intergenerational tastes.

Reflections

After a number of experiences with this baptismal liturgy, there has been generally very positive feedback. The families of the newly baptised have appreciated the congregation's efforts to make the celebration a personal welcome. Many of their friends and family members who did not have a strong church connection expressed surprise and pleasure that they felt comfortable during the service. They also felt they had started to understand what baptism meant.

The regular parishioners enjoyed the opportunity for a liturgical blow-out. They were proud of their parish and felt that they had witnessed to a wider community. The liturgy is labour intensive and takes time to prepare. However, through the labour some of the intensity of family hopes for the future can be expressed.

Lent

During the season of Lent, the message and the practice of the church are often at odds. On the one hand Lent is proclaimed as a time for cutting back, for a return to simplicity of living, for renewed relationships with God, and for a restoration of balance within ourselves. On the other hand Lent is often a time for the church to make extra demands for more time spent in prayer, educational programs, and work for social justice. Perhaps if we did cut back in one area then we would have time to spend in the other; however, the Lenten admonitions usually end up sounding like "Do more!" Yet the message of Lent is just what we and our consumptive, workaholic society need most. If we add things on to our already busy lives, then we are just compounding our problems. The theme of Lenten liturgy is "Be more, with less."

Being more means acknowledging our total dependence upon God, and being refreshed by God's gracious goodness. We can be more if we depend upon God's promises to us, and find in those promises the motivation to be faithful to one another and to the created order we inhabit.

Lenten liturgy is not a time for extravaganza. A few simple touches and variations are all that are required. We need to be directed towards our failings as a human race and we also need to be directed towards God's promises of renewal and restoration. Lenten liturgy should allow that journey to take place with a minimal amount of suggestion. Here are some ways those suggestions were made in the context of the gathering rite.

The Masks of Mardi Gras

One thing we do during Lent is to come to terms with our real selves, and this, as we know, includes a shadow or hidden self. If we try to repress this dark side of our nature and pretend that it isn't there, we end up doing a great deal of personal and social damage under the guise of self-righteousness. Mardi Gras festivals are one way societies have made an outlet for expressing "the lord of misrule." People dress up to express an aspect of themselves they would not otherwise reveal. In some Caribbean festivals of Mardi Gras the costumes are cleverly concealed political satire.

When we put on a mask we reveal as well as conceal. When we take it off we are both the person underneath as well as the person who dared to put it on. Mardi Gras is a time for costume and becoming someone different. Lent is a time for unmasking and becoming whole. One year our church members with roots in the Caribbean helped us to celebrate Mardi Gras in the style of the islands. There was much costume-making for weeks in advance and then a party was held for all ages. The next Sunday was Lent 1, and we picked up the theme of masks in the liturgy.

We began the liturgy quietly with a litany of penitence and intercession. The first petition made reference to our theme: "Lord, your ways are not our ways; your thoughts are not our thoughts; what to us seems like eternity is only a moment to you. In this moment of eternity, we come before you in humility; we now remove all our masks and reveal all those things hidden in our hearts, those things that you alone already know." As the people sang a refrain to this and the following petitions they were sprinkled with water as a symbol of God's renewing power.

The gospel was dramatized at the font. Three splendid masks had been procured from a theatre company to represent the three temptations. As Satan tempted Jesus, he offered her (played by a girl!) a mask. She took the mask and put it on. After all, these are real temptations arising as much from within as from without. During this moment of decision members of the congregation shouted out a repetition of the temptation: "Command, command, command" for the first temptation. The children replied, "No, no, no!" and Jesus put aside the mask. This was repeated for each temptation. At the end of the gospel the masks were taken to the front of the church where they became a focal point for the homily, and remained as visible reminders of our need to put away our masks and seek authenticity and wholeness in our lives. The joyful festivity of Mardi Gras gave way to the simplicity of Lent.

Renewing Waters

The First Sunday of Lent (year B) has readings which allude to the covenants between God and humanity through the sign of water. After the flood, the rainbow appears (Genesis 9:8–17); 1 Peter 3: 18–22 speaks directly about baptism and the forgiveness of sins; the gospel is the story of the baptism of Jesus (Mark 1: 9–15).

Water is essential to life. Margaret Mead, the anthropologist, boiled down the social, political, and ecological mission of the world to providing safe, clean drinking water to every human being.

As people entered the church building they saw a sign: "This week we begin our journey towards Easter. As our community gathers we keep a quiet time to think about God's loving forgiveness promised in baptism. We lay our lives before God who calls us to bring renewal and peace to our broken world."

A gentle chant was being sung in parts. ("Bless the Lord, my soul, and bless God's holy name. Bless the Lord, my soul, God comes to set us free.") Slides of lakes, rivers, waterfalls, rain, rainbows, and water in many other forms were projected above the altar. Then as the chant drew to a close, the congregation was sprinkled with water.

As a counterpoint to the water imagery at the altar's base was a stark arrangement of dry sticks in a bed of sand.

This theme was developed through the music with such choices as "Joy shall come even to the wilderness" and the Strathdees' "With the Lord as my guide" as a dismissal.

On Going Home

While not wanting to load extra obligations upon people during Lent, we did want to offer ideas that could bring the suggestions of the liturgy into a domestic setting. Using the excellent book, *To Dance with God*, by Gertrud Mueller Nelson, several parents developed the following sheet for take-home use.

SOME IDEAS AND ACTIVITIES FOR LENT

Lent, Literally, Means Spring

In this country, Lent does not coincide with the balmy, blossomy part of spring but rather with a time of planting, rooting and waiting — a time to get ready to grow. This image of Lent might be captured by one or more of the following:

— planting a dry branch and hanging on it one paper blossom each day until Easter.
— planting bulbs in a pot — begonia tubers are readily available at this time of year. (Colourful planters can be made from the bottom of plastic containers. Fruit baskets can be lined with plastic and filled with earth.) Bulbs must be kept in the dark, tended carefully, brought out into the light when shoots appear.
— making an arrangement of twigs and dried weeds. As Lent progresses, add spring greens, pussywillows, and finally flowers.

Lent is a Time of Reconciliation

It is a time for binding together again, with God's help, the fragments of our lives, our relationships and our world. This journey towards wholeness might be represented by:

— cutting a map of the world, or a photograph of the planet, into 40 jigsaw-like pieces and reassembling it, one piece a day. The region of the world restored each day might be remembered in family prayers.

Special Meals

— can be times of reconciliation within our family.
— can be simple without being austere.
— eating as a family without distractions can strengthen family ties.
— intentionally planning meals "for a small planet" can bring the whole human family closer together.
— giving up unhelpful mealtime habits such as nagging can help re-establish family bonds.
— giving up an unhealthy favourite food can be a step towards reconciliation with our often maligned bodies.
— giving up luxuries, or replacing store-bought items with home-made ones (cookies, pizza, etc., made by family members working together) might be a step towards reconciliation with our hungry world. Money saved can be sent to local food banks or to agencies which support famine relief efforts.

The Paschal Celebration

Palm Sunday marks the beginning of Holy Week and the commemoration of the passion, death, and resurrection of Jesus. Modern liturgists encourage us to think of those events as part of one single commemoration of Jesus' victory over sin and death. In the past, isolating the events has lead to an unequal emphasis on the cross with insufficient attention being given to the empty tomb. This rethinking of the meaning of the paschal mystery is also helpful when planning liturgies for young people. The notion of "sad days" and "happy days" is rather bewildering for most children — we suspect for most adults as well. In our parish we chose to keep the passion and resurrection in close proximity through the use of continuing symbols and movement. In this way, while we stood beneath the cross, we never forgot that the empty tomb lay ahead, and in the Easter garden we still saw the cross before us.

As will be seen, the planning for three liturgies in one week is an enormous logistical task, and we developed the sequence over a two-year period: Good Friday the first year, with the addition of Palm Sunday and Easter Day in the second year. Although the core planning group of four people was the co-ordinating team, each liturgy had its own group of hands-on people. In fact, everyone who had taken some part in the liturgy in the past year could count on helping out! These are the most labour-intensive liturgies of the year — and the most rewarding. We should also note that in our parish the celebrations that included young people paralleled the principal services of Holy Week. Thus, we could not plan any participation for the children at the important celebrations of Maundy Thursday and Easter Eve. Each church should look at the needs of all its members when planning Holy Week and Easter.

The Sunday of the Passion: Palm Sunday

The new name for Palm Sunday emphasizes its primary focus on the whole passion of Jesus. Thus, the old triumphalist liturgies of the past which focussed solely on Jesus the triumphant king need to be seriously rethought. The first thing that impressed us about the story was the sense of movement: riding, running, shouting, sitting, waiting. So we used a variety of locations inside and outside the church and asked the people to move from place to place as the liturgies unfolded. That physical movement helped us to identify with the very physical narrative unfolding before us.

The second component which we saw in the readings was the use of signs and symbols. Seeing and believing was such a consistent theme that we decided to use a series of strong visual symbols which would reappear and change as we walked through the story. This helped us link together the three liturgies in a graphic way which was impossible with mere words.

The Palm Sunday rite falls into three main parts:

1. *The Liturgy of the Palms* — the reading of the account of the entry into Jerusalem, the blessing of palms, and the procession with branches.
2. *The Proclamation of the Word* — the readings and the dramatization of the passion gospel.
3. *The Celebration of the Eucharist* — beginning with the offertory and preparation of the gifts.

THE LITURGY OF THE PALMS

The first part of the liturgy took place in a school playground across from the church. As people arrived they were given palm branches. These were real branches that could be waved, not single leaves or palm crosses. Many countries use local trees for branches; North Americans might wish to use a mixture of pine branches and flowering branches forced for the day. One year we adapted a Dutch custom which symbolized Jesus' words that he wished he could gather us all up as a hen gathers up her chicks. The children and their families had been asked to bake brioches in the shape of chickens. These were now mounted on poles with red and purple ribbons (red being the colour of sacrifice, and purple the colour of kingship).

On another occasion, we asked a carpenter in the parish to make three-foot-high wooden crosses to which banners could be affixed. On Palm Sunday they had red and purple banners, on Good Friday they were bare wooden crosses, and on Easter Day they had gold and white pennants. That continuity of symbol joined the liturgies in a striking visual metaphor. Everyone, young and old, should have something to carry in the procession.

The gospel of the palms was read, and the palms and banners were blessed with a short prayer. Led by servers and a small band of teenagers playing flute, horn, and trombone, the procession moved off rather informally but with great enthusiasm to the church door. A repeated Hosanna refrain was sung. Music sung outdoors should be simple and rhythmic. Instruments are not essential — strong unaccompanied singing with percussion (drums and tambourines) is often easier to keep together. A familiar hymn such as "All glory, laud and honour" would work equally well but will be difficult for the children. The essence of this rite is to capture the sense of excitement and physical movement which characterizes the narrative. This is the first stage of our journey to the empty tomb. Some practical considerations: Keep this section short, at least if you are facing an unpredictable northern spring. Start on time (no matter who's not there), do it without long explanations, and reflect on it later in the service. In practice, most congregations will arrive at the church and then have to regather outside.

The Proclamation of the Word

The procession stopped at the door of the church where the children discovered a rough wooden cross lying on the sidewalk (a seven-foot-high cross made from 2x4 is a good size). From the church steps, a teenager read the short reading from Isaiah which prophesied the death which Jesus accepted when he entered Jerusalem. The cross made an immediate effect on all present as the children were asked to raise it and carry it on their shoulders into the church (discreet adult assistance is desirable to ensure safety). Although the mood of the liturgy was beginning to change, it remained strong and forceful. The great hymn of the church of Philippi is intended as the second reading (Philippians 2.5–11), but we decided to restore it to what it once was, a powerful hymn praising the sacrifice of Christ. The most familiar metrical version is "All praise to thee." There are also several modern adaptations available which may be sung to the tune "Sine Nomine."

Accompanied by the full organ and all the instruments, the people entered the church and processed to the front where the collect or prayer of the day was read. The people then sat and joined hands to keep a three- or four-minute silence. This had both a practical and a liturgical effect: coats could be jettisoned, palms laid aside, hands warmed up. Gradually, the silence deepened, and we finally felt that we could corporately begin the passion gospel. The effect of silence is surprising and even young people will respond to it if everyone actively joins in. (Remember too that real silence is not attainable on earth: radiators will always bang, someone will blow their nose and somewhere a child will always be crying. Persevere!) As the silence continued, the children set up the cross so that it was upright in the centre.

The dramatic reading of the passion gospel presumes a creative use of the space in the church. In our parish we are blessed with a small congregation in a large building! That allows us to move around from place to place in the building. About a hundred people can sit on the wide chancel steps facing out towards the nave.

Sitting close together gives a real sense of community which is enhanced when the people have to play the crowd in the story on Palm Sunday. At the bottom of the steps is a wide space which is the stage for the passion story. Everyone can see easily and is very close to the action. The location of the passion gospel reading will depend on the space available and the creativity of the readers and actors. Our method of dramatizing the gospel arose out of the physical layout of our church building. Planners are invited to walk around their buildings and imagine the most dramatic and non-traditional uses for doors, lecterns, steps, windows, furniture. Let the space create the drama.

ALTERNATE SUGGESTIONS

a)   The people can sit closely together in the front pews of the nave and the choir stalls. The narrator stands at the lectern or pulpit with the cross in the centre of the chancel steps. The actors use the main and side aisles while readers stand up wherever they are sitting in the nave.

b)   The procession can go first to the parish hall if it has a large space available for the dramatization. Circular seating works especially well. A proscenium stage should be avoided as it will be difficult for the people to take their part in the reading.

It should be noted that the passion gospel here is treated as a dramatic reading, not as a fully staged passion play. The latter is of course possible, but time is a consideration, as is the danger of overemphasizing this part of the liturgy. In most instances, the straightforward narrative of the scriptures has a power which nothing can replace. The narrator reads the story. The parts of Pilate and Jesus are read by two children who simply stand and face each other when they read. Other parts are read by children from wherever they are sitting. The part of the crowd is taken by the people. Repeating each shout three times gives the crowd more life.

As the story unfolds, children bring forward a succession of symbols: a purple cloak, dice, a crown of thorns, a pitcher of water and basin, a hammer and three nails — the narrative will suggest the appropriate sign. The child simply shows the object to the people and places it at the foot of the upright cross. Some simple actions can be mimed: as we hear how Pilate washed his hands, water can be poured from the pitcher into the jug. The card with the name of Jesus can be placed at the top of the cross. The following is an excerpt from the passion gospel of Mark in year B:

(*All stand.* CHILDREN *show the cup, hammer and nails, and dice to the people and place them at the foot of the cross.*)

And they brought him to the place called Golgotha (which means the place of a skull). And they offered him wine mingled with myrrh; but he did not take it. And they crucified him, and divided his garments among them, casting lots for them, to decide what each should take. And it was the third hour, when they crucified him.

(CHILD *shows the inscription to the people and places it on the cross. A server comes forward to help.*)

And the inscription of the charge against him read, "The King of the Jews." And with him they crucified two robbers, one on his right and one on his left. And those who passed by derided him, wagging their heads, and saying,

MOCKER 1: Ha! You who would destroy the temple and build it in three days, save yourself, and come down from the cross!

PEOPLE: Come down from the cross! Come down from the cross! Come down from the cross!

Although many churches have quasi-dramatic reading of the passion gospel, the rite here allows for a complete participation of all present, and for a very simple but effective role for even the youngest non-reader.

The homily, the prayers of the people, and the exchange of the peace complete this section of the liturgy. Because the gospel carries us so far away imaginatively, it is important that the homily and prayers establish a link between the story and the realities of people's lives.

THE CELEBRATION OF THE EUCHARIST

Again, the physical layout of our building allowed us to form once more our procession with banners and move to a third location where the eucharist was celebrated. This enabled us to refocus attention on the altar. The children carried the bread and wine and all the chalices and baskets necessary, as well as taking up the collection. In other churches the space will help suggest how this final part of the liturgy should be shaped. The cross could be carried up to stand behind the altar with the banners. Because we were unable to integrate the children into the Maundy Thursday rite which commemorates Christ's washing of the disciples' feet and the last supper, care was taken to choose songs at the offertory, breaking of the bread, and communion which placed those events in the paschal sequence. The texts also were chosen or adapted so that the promise of Easter was always the concluding theme.

As is usual in our celebrations, the eucharistic prayer was sung by the celebrant while the people offered a sung acclamation after each section. An attempt was made to bring the liturgy from the shouts of joy of the palm procession to a quiet time of reflection during the communion. The liturgy ended quietly with no music, as if it was unresolved and would continue at the next gathering.

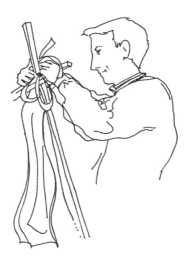

The Celebration of the Lord's Passion: Good Friday

For many centuries, there was no liturgical celebration of Christ's death. The churches were left bare and undecorated on Thursday night, and everyone closed their doors in quiet remembrance of the time when Jesus hung on the cross. Gradually, the liturgy developed to meet the needs of the churches who wanted to gather and make their recollection collectively. However, we do well to remember the quiet, domestic mood which shaped the commemoration of Good Friday for many centuries.

For our liturgy, we adapted the structure of the traditional stations of the cross. The devotion began as part of the medieval pilgrimage to Jerusalem. Visitors wanted to see the places associated with the final hours of Jesus' life. The last part of their pilgrimage, which may have begun thousands of miles away, would be to physically walk with Jesus and remember those dark hours. Pilgrims still do that today, and the devotion is still popular in many Catholic churches. The principal appeal of the devotion is its sheer physicality. We walk and look and touch. We felt that children could enter into the story more fully if we gave them a hands-on physical kind of liturgy. The resulting format has proved very flexible over the last few years. Finally, we should note that this event has more of the feel of a popular personal devotion than of formal worship. Perhaps as in no other liturgy presented here are the lines between worship and play so deliberately obscured.

That experiential approach also allows people, both children and adults, to find their own level of involvement. This is particularly important if the narrative is felt to be too powerful or even frightening for children. Through the very real involvement of both young and old, parents and children, we take possession of this crucial part of the Christian story. So too we can relate the events and feelings to our own lives and the lives around us. The following outline provides the pattern of the liturgy. In various years some stations have been omitted or combined or new ones developed. The format is particularly good for gradual development over several years. Each station had a planner who facilitated the activity; some members took on responsibility for more than one station.

As we moved from one station to another we sang unaccompanied rounds:

1) "Jesus, we adore you" with the following words:

   Jesus, let me walk with you,
   Jesus let me die with you,
   Let me rise with you.

2) "Amazing Grace"

3) Tune: Tallis's Canon

   O Jesus, let me walk with you,
   O Jesus, let me die with you,
   O Jesus, let me rest with you,
   O Jesus, let me rise with you.

STATION ONE — JESUS IS CONDEMNED BY PILATE

The trial before Pilate is easily the most dramatic story in the whole bible, and so we asked the children to dramatize it. Once again the people were encouraged to sit on the chancel steps and take part in the action. The link with the Palm Sunday gospel provided continuity between the liturgies over the week. The informal setting also helped people to feel engaged and part of the community.

In a very informal way, the leader rehearsed the music with the people and then explained that we were going to re-enact the trial when Pilate asked the people to choose between Jesus and Barabbas. We asked for boys and girls to play Jesus and Barabbas. Each of them was guarded by two soldiers who were given spears, and three other soldiers who held the purple robe, the reed, and the crown of thorns (an ivy vine plaited in a circle). With Jesus on one side and Barabbas on the other, the leader told the people that they were the crowd and were to choose Barabbas and condemn Jesus with "Crucify him!" The leader threw on a black cloak and became Pilate. A narrator sitting with the people began the story:

NARRATOR: Jesus stood before the governor. Now at the festival the governor was accustomed to release a prisoner for the crowd, anyone whom they wanted. At that time they had a notorious prisoner called Barabbas. So after they had gathered, Pilate said to them,

PILATE: Whom do you want me to release for you, Barabbas or Jesus who is called the Messiah?

PEOPLE: Barabbas! Barabbas! Barabbas!

PILATE: Then what should I do with Jesus who is called the Messiah?

PEOPLE: Let him be crucified! Let him be crucified! Let him be crucified!

PILATE: Why, what evil has he done?

PEOPLE: Let him be crucified! Let him be crucified! Let him be crucified!
(*Barabbas is released by Pilate and the soldiers and returns to the crowd.*)

NARRATOR: So he released Barabbas for them and after flogging Jesus, he handed him over to be crucified. Then the soldiers of the governor took Jesus ... and they gathered the whole cohort around him.
(The cloak and crown are put on Jesus and the reed is put in his hand.)
They stripped him and put a purple robe on him, and after twisting some thorns into a crown, they put it on his head. They put a reed in his right hand and knelt before him and mocked him saying,

PEOPLE *(led by Pilate)*: Hail, King of the Jews! Hail, King of the Jews! Hail, King of the Jews!

NARRATOR: They spat on him and took the reed and struck him on the head. After mocking him, they stripped him of the robe and put his own clothes on him. Then they led him away to crucify him.
{The crown, cloak, and reed are taken from Jesus.)

The drama was not realistic in the way a stage play would be. However, the unfair release of Barabbas and the mocking of Jesus by the crowd were made all the more poignant by the fact that children were representing the characters and that the bullying could well have been seen in any playground. The music began and we moved off to the next station without comment.

Station Two — Jesus Carries His Cross

The procession led to a meeting room in the church basement. The leader introduced the activity by saying that we were going to make crosses to help us remember Jesus' death. Strips of wooden lathing had been cut in lengths of 10" and 5" in sufficient quantities that would allow each child to make a cross. Tacks and rough string were used to attach the pieces. As the activity drew to a close, the leader asked the children to help assemble the large wooden cross which had been used on Palm Sunday, the beams of which now had to be fitted together and tied. The Palm Sunday processional crosses, now stripped of any decoration, were also given out to be carried. This final preparation helped to refocus attention after all the hammering. Some of the children shouldered the large cross. Others took up the smaller processional crosses. Everyone had their personal cross. The procession moved off to the next station which was outdoors. It should be noted that very little needed to be said about the making of the crosses. The symbol has great strength, and, by making their own miniature crosses, the children took possession of that all-important sign.

STATION THREE — JESUS MEETS SIMON OF CYRENE

Almost as soon as we were outside on the sidewalk, we stopped and asked the children to put down the large cross and feel the pavement. The leader paraphrased the story of Simon: Jesus was too weak to carry his cross, so Simon was forced to pick it up. The leader then asked other children, especially the very young, to take up the cross and continue the procession.

STATION FOUR — JESUS MEETS THE WOMEN OF JERUSALEM

The fourth station has always varied each time that we have done the liturgy. At this station, we try to link Jesus' fall and his words to the threatened women of Jerusalem with the oppression and injustice in the world today. The leader first asked a mother to read the story in Luke 23:27–31. Jesus' words are blunt and shocking, and we have tried to connect his care for the weak and helpless with situations that the children could remember and relate to.

One year the station was made under a stop sign which had been recently erected after a child had been hit by a car in front of the church. The relationship to Jesus' sufferings was direct and uncomplicated.

Another year we stopped in a nearby school yard. The leader asked the children to tell us about the bullying and hurting which they had seen among children at school. Again, the connection with Jesus' passion was simple.

On another occasion a member of the parish who works in a clothing depot for the homeless spoke about his experiences with refugees and street people.

Another year we stopped in a nearby park which was frequented by street people and drug-users. The leader asked the children to tell us about all the fun things that happened in the park. She then asked them to tell us about the problems they had seen. The observations included drug and alcohol abuse, but also the plight of lonely children and bullying.

In each case, the stories of hurt and injustice came naturally out of the participants' experiences, and, in each case, the cross seemed to carry our witness and concern.

STATION FIVE — JESUS IS CRUCIFIED

The procession now re-entered the church and gathered in a large open area at the back. (We found the area around the font to be the most practical.) The cross was laid on the floor and the leader asked a teenager to read one of the accounts of the crucifixion (Matthew 27:33–40 is appropriate). Without any graphic description, the leader showed the people a large rail spike and passed it around so that everyone could feel its weight and sharpness. The children were then asked to hammer in three smaller nails on the two arms and foot of the cross. Each child was given an opportunity to tap the nails with the hammer. Again, no explanation was needed: the juxtaposition of the scriptural reading and the activity was sufficient. It should be noted that children's responses to these actions are neither solemn nor macabre. They respond with enthusiasm and energy because they are doing something. The task is tackled with verve and determination: we should not try to "devotionalize" it, or the physicality of the story will be lost.

The cross was then raised by the children and placed in its stand. Again, adults do well to stand back and let the young people struggle to find a co-operative way to place the cross in an upright position. At this point, the leader showed the children a placard reading, "This is Jesus." In various years, we have tried in different ways to connect the name of Jesus with the names of others for whom he died.

One year, we asked the children and the adults to write their own names on adhesive labels which were then stuck on the placard around the name Jesus.

On another occasion, a parishioner who had a connection with human rights organizations in South Africa spoke very simply and briefly about the young people being detained in prison. He had a list of names of detainees and was able to say that if we wrote to those prisoners they would receive the cards. So everyone chose a name and made a card with a simple message of hope. Those cards were delivered to the prisoners through a church agency.

Another year, we invited a family of refugees from Latin America to speak about the sufferings of the people they knew and loved. They gave us many names, and each of those names was inscribed beside the name of Jesus.

On another Good Friday, we were asked for the names of those who we knew were sick or lonely or suffering, especially children. Those names too became a circle around the name of Jesus.

The activity of writing helped to focus the attention of the young participants and gradually the group became quite quiet. The placard was placed on the cross, and the leader asked everyone to kneel quietly around the cross. The silence was profound.

STATION SIX — JESUS IS BURIED

The next leader then briefly described how Jesus' friends and family took his body down from the cross, and took it with a burial shroud and spices to the tomb in the garden. The children were given various objects to carry: a large white sheet as the shroud, an icon with the face of Jesus, and five or six dishes containing fragrant cooking herbs such as cinnamon, allspice, whole cloves, nutmeg, and mace. Quietly singing our round and carrying the processional crosses, we processed to a side aisle where a small papier-mâché model of the tomb stood on a table draped in purple. A painting of grey clouds hung behind it. This tomb would later be the centre of our flowering Easter garden, but at the moment it was dark and bare.

The children spread out the sheet on the floor and sat around the edge. The leader was someone who had an experience of a burial: on one occasion, it was someone who had recently organized a relative's funeral; on another occasion, the facilitator was a nurse who had to prepare patients after they had died. In each case, the speaker spoke simply but accurately about washing and dressing a body for burial. As she did, she placed the icon of Jesus in the centre of the sheet.

The leader then described how Jesus' friends wrapped his body in a shroud with many sweet-smelling spices. The bowls of spices were passed around so that everyone could smell the different aromas. Then each child was asked to throw a pinch of each spice onto the icon as if they were preparing Jesus for burial. Then the children were asked to wrap the icon up in the sheet with the spices and place it in the tomb. The stone was rolled over the opening and a moment of silence was kept. The bare processional crosses were left standing around the tomb. We then began our round again and processed to the final station.

STATION SEVEN — JESUS' PROMISE OF EASTER

Our final station was an attempt to look ahead to the joy of Easter and keep the resurrection before our eyes even in the quietness of Good Friday. Hanging above the altar in the sanctuary in our parish is a large cross with the figure of Jesus. It is not Jesus in death but reigning triumphant from the cross. The children were asked to sit in the centre aisle and look closely at the cross.

"What is different about this cross and the one we carried today?"

"It is painted with beautiful colours ... it has flowers growing from it."

"What is different about Jesus?"

"He's wearing a white robe ... and a golden crown."

"What about his hands?"

"They're not nailed to the cross ... he's making that blessing sign with his two fingers."

"What about his eyes?"

"They're open ... he's alive not dead."

"Who's he looking at?"

"Me ... us."

The cross thus became a powerful link between the darkness of Good Friday and the light of Easter Day. Like Jesus' friends, we all promised to meet back at the garden in three days to visit the tomb again.

The use of our sanctuary cross is a good example of how we let our church building shape the visual symbols of our liturgy. Other churches will have equally strong images: a stained-glass window, a sculpture, a gravestone with an Easter image. Or someone may have a cross or icon or reproduction. Better still, an artist or the children themselves might paint or sculpt a representation which speaks of the promise of Easter.

CONCLUDING ACTIVITY

The liturgy was designed to last about 75 minutes. After the final station, we invited all of the children to come to the parish hall for hot cross buns, the traditional Good Friday breakfast. The adults had tea and coffee, and we kept the gathering rather low key so as not to upstage the grand Easter breakfast planned for Sunday. On one occasion we made Easter cards for prisoners of conscience. We also invited the children to help begin the preparations for Easter by making Easter eggs. Hard boiled eggs had been dyed, and the children were given markers, crayon, fabric, glitter, and sequins and asked to create. If they were not returning for Easter, they were allowed to take their eggs home. The others were told to come back to find their eggs in the Easter garden. Thus, the final image that they carried away with them was the promise of something splendid yet to come.

The Sunday of the Resurrection: Easter Day

As the resurrection is the centre of our faith, so Easter Day is the centre of the church year. In a very real sense, the Sundays leading up to it are a preparation, and the Sundays which follow it are a response. It goes without saying that the liturgy on this day has to be the best that we can offer to the risen Lord. Two factors need to be taken into account when planning the Easter liturgy. First, Easter Day like Christmas will draw many people who may have only a very slight connection with the church. We may not know what motivates them, but we have a special pastoral obligation to gather them into the celebration. The second factor regards over-blown liturgies. The celebration of Easter runs a real risk of being an overwhelming crush of trumpets and lilies. This triumphalism can be wonderfully exciting and theatrical, but we should try to keep the human element in perspective. The story is a remarkably simple one, and we should keep our focus closely on those early morning encounters with the risen Lord.

It should be noted that the Easter Vigil on Saturday evening is the liturgy which has the richest possibilities for liturgical creativity, and many churches may find that

rite the obvious place to focus their Easter celebration. Many of the ideas outlined here
for Easter morning would easily adapt to that magnificent liturgy.

THE GATHERING OF THE COMMUNITY

The preparation for the Easter liturgy had as its visual goal an image of transformation
to a new life. We had left the worshippers on Good Friday with the darkening image
of the tomb. Only the glitter of a few sequins on the Easter eggs gave some premoni-
tion of what lay ahead. For Easter morning, each of the symbols which we had used
were decorated with great care. As people came into the church, they saw the old with
new eyes. The bare processional crosses now had white and gold banners attached.
The large wooden cross had flowered; it had become a tree of life with branches and
blossoms. Even the crown of thorns had become a circlet of flowers. The baskets of
decorated eggs lay at the foot of the cross. The tomb now stood in a miniature garden
with a glorious rainbow arching above it. And the tomb itself lay open and empty: the
icon was gone. The gathering became an exploration of these wonderful things, and
both the children and the adults were delighted to find that the hard symbols of Good
Friday had become something beautiful. Thus, the first activities were touching,
smelling, pointing, and laughing. At the same time, the setting was intimate: the Easter
garden stood in the same place that the creche had at Christmas. We began with an
Easter carol, just as we began with a noel in December. The atmosphere was personal
and familial. The clergy and servers joined us quietly without any formal entrance
ceremony.

The reader of the gospel then gathered the children around the garden, and
together they pointed out all the changes that occurred. And the greatest change was
that the tomb was empty. Almost as if a story-book was opening, the Easter gospel
began. The story of the women seeing the empty grave and Mary Magdalene's encounter with Jesus unfolded. At last, we and the women at the tomb were commissioned to
go and tell the world of the resurrection of Jesus. We gathered up our banners, the
eggs, the candles, "burial" cloths, and books for the altar, we lit candles and incense,
and began a joyful procession through the church. The important factor here is that
we began quietly and allowed the liturgy to recreate the first intimate contact with the
risen Jesus. Then the celebration began to expand, and the bells began to ring. We
were embarking on a new journey: a journey to proclaim the gospel of the empty
tomb.

THE PROCLAMATION OF THE WORD

The two New Testament lections were read by teenagers. The normal sequence of the readings was altered in this liturgy because it seemed appropriate to read the gospel beside the tomb. The readings from Acts and Paul are responses to the Easter news, and so the news of the resurrection seemed to spread through the disciples and out into the world. During the homily, the preacher picked up the story of the first Easter again. We were the women at the tomb. We had come and told Peter and John and the other disciples the most incredible story:

"What would you do if you were Peter and John?"

"Go and look for ourselves!"

The preacher selected two boys and told them to run to the tomb as fast as they could and look inside.

"GO!"

The two boys thundered through the church to the side aisle. The preacher shouted to them:

"What do you see?"

"Nothing!"

"What?!"

"NOTHING!!"

"Run back and tell us! !"

And like Peter and John running from the tomb, the swifter runner reached the preacher in a photo-finish.

"What did you see?"

"*(Gasp)* ... we ... *(gasp)* ... saw ... *(gasp)* ... empty!"

No painting, no narrative, no discourse could make the excitement of the first Easter come to life better than those two panting boys, each trying to catch his breath *and* be the first to tell what they saw. The preacher then challenged us to keep that excitement in our baptismal commission to live the new life of the gospel.

To emphasize that challenge, we renewed the vows we had taken at baptism. There are several versions of this profession of faith based on the Apostles' Creed. Additional questions and answers can be appended to the sequence. To remind us of our own baptism into the death and resurrection of Jesus, the celebrant and the children walked through the church sprinkling all the people with water. A bowl or vat of water and pine branches are a traditional way of splashing water liturgically. The joyful waterplay naturally turned into a happy exchange of the peace.

THE CELEBRATION OF THE EUCHARIST

Once again, the children were responsible for the presentation of the gifts of bread, wine, and money at the altar. At this time the baskets of Easter eggs were laid at the foot of the altar. Care was taken so that the children could come right up to the altar to assist the preparation. A stool was placed in front so that even the smallest could climb up to see the top of the table. Several children helped to arrange the baskets of bread. Others helped to pour the wine and water into the cup. Our parish uses incense as a symbol of prayer rising to heaven. The children helped to pour the incense on the coals, and the celebrant not only censed the altar and sanctuary but came down into the body of the church so that every worshipper felt that their prayer was caught up in the cloud. The eucharistic prayer and communion shaped a quiet time of reflection in the liturgy. The final prayers were closed with a brief but happy "Thanks be to God!"

For this day, a special brunch was laid out for the congregation in the parish hall. Traditional Easter foods from many countries and cultures loaded the table. The Easter eggs were distributed, and the community continued its celebration with convivial table fellowship.

The Fifty Days of Easter

Perhaps the most important challenge which the liturgical movement has posed is the restoration of the Easter season, the "Greater Fifty" from Easter to Pentecost. The early church kept the season with enthusiasm: hospitality, singing, feasting. In most churches today, however, Easter is the end not the beginning of a cycle. All of the creative energy and devotion which went into Lent and Holy Week suddenly seem to disappear. Liturgical exhaustion is everywhere. It's no accident that the week after Easter is traditionally called Low Sunday!

This problem should tell us that our familiar emphasis on Lent and Holy Week has unbalanced the Easter celebration. We have spent 40 days in the desert and beneath the cross; we now have 50 days to walk in the garden and on the shores of Galilee. The challenge is all the more urgent in that, where we had rich liturgical traditions for Holy Week, we have used very little from the medieval church which does not focus almost exclusively on the cross. Thus, we have much work to do to make the paschal season as compelling as the 40 days of Lenten preparation.

Our first resource as always is the rich scriptural selection for the season. The lectionary for Easter has a pattern unlike the rest of the church year. The Old Testament lesson is replaced by a continuous reading of the Acts of the Apostles. In years A and B, we encounter the accounts of the first mission of Peter and the disciples in Jerusalem. Year C introduces Paul the Apostle and the mission to the Gentiles. The second New Testament reading is given over to the witness of apostolic writers other than Paul. Year A draws from 1 Peter while year B reads from 1 John. All of these readings give us the primary theme of the growth of the church through the apostles' witness to the resurrection. Year C takes us into the visionary world of Revelation. The gospel of John provides the final reading for all three years. These readings give the Easter season a special character which we should try to enhance and emphasize in our liturgical planning.

We should next look at some of the continuing symbols which may give us a visual focus for the season. Perhaps the most important is the paschal candle. This large candle is traditionally decorated and lit on Easter Eve as a symbol of the light of Christ triumphing over the darkness of sin and death. It burns until Pentecost and all other candles are lit from it. Many of the Sundays continue to develop the imagery of the light of Christ. Easter 2 and 6 (year C) both recreate the vision of light in Revelation, and the paschal candle is a logical focus for the liturgy. Indeed, the whole series of readings from Revelation calls out for artistic representation. A changing montage or installation of symbols around the candle could prove effective. On one occasion the children in our parish created a mural of their city as the heavenly city which became a frontal for the altar. On another occasion, the reading was the temple of "living stones." The children wrote their names on shoe-boxes covered with brown paper. Using a cornerstone with the name Jesus, the children built quite a substantial wall.

The Easter garden can also continue to grow and flourish during the season. Like the creche during the Christmas season, it is a natural focus for intimate activity especially with children. On Easter 4 the theme is Jesus the Good Shepherd. One year we asked the children to bring the sheep from their nativity scenes at home. That Sunday the liturgy began at the garden and a shepherd figure and a whole flock of sheep was placed among the plants and flowers. Several Sundays use natural images which could also be part of the garden. Easter 6 (A) has "I am the Vine; you are the branches" as its gospel. Easter 6 (C) describes the tree of life in its New Testament reading.

The baptismal font is another important focus in the Easter season. In fact, we could say that the whole season is an extended meditation on how we live out our baptismal commission as an Easter people. The readings from 1 Peter in year A give us a strong baptismal message which could be underlined by liturgical waterplay at the font; washing and drinking are significant themes which could be developed.

The Easter readings also give us an opportunity to renew or introduce parts of the liturgical action. The exchange of the peace figures strongly in the appearances of Jesus, and the rite could be emphasized in a more intentional way. The travellers to Emmaus allow us to focus on the gift of bread as a symbol of physical and spiritual nourishment. Bread-baking is a wonderful preparatory activity for the liturgy.

Music too can play a significant role in a number of ways. The readings from Revelation in year C are full of musical imagery. If we believe that music is truly a gateway to the sacred then we are halfway to John's little door into heaven. It would be a worthwhile project to take the readings as music dramas and use song and percussion instruments to tell their stories. The children can make instruments as well: water glasses and rhythm instruments can be the basis of a beautiful soundscape. Nor should we forget the possibilities for creative composition offered by the Orff method. This type of music teaching encourages children to enhance their musicality through creativity and improvisation. The use of bells, drums, xylophones, and recorders can create wonderful music which the children can write themselves. On several occasions we have begun our liturgies with a session of music-making which the children have assembled and performed themselves. An Orff teacher will be an invaluable resource in planning the music of the liturgy.

The Easter season can also provide the focus for preparation for a special event. Ascension Day is one of the midweek feasts which are suggested as a date for a parish day. The event would help give the season a sense of anticipation. The previous Sundays could be used to prepare for the central themes: the completion of Jesus' earthly ministry and the waiting for the Spirit. A parish confirmation might well be part of the Easter season.

The Easter season closes with Pentecost and the celebration of the coming of the Spirit. In many parishes Pentecost will be a baptismal festival (suggestions for baptismal liturgies are found on pages 89–98). Our liturgies on Pentecost should focus on responsive prayer with God. On one occasion, the gathering rite consisted of a simple repeated invocation, "Come, O Holy Spirit, Come." As people took their seats, they gradually became part of the quiet, pulsing music. On the wall, above the altar, a projector continuously showed slides of children's art depicting light and the coming of the Spirit. Many of them were abstract and just pure colour. The music and art permitted a real mood of reflection and expectation to be created. The use of abstract colours alerted us to the extraordinarily flexible imagery which we use in our conception of God the Holy Spirit. The Holy Spirit is most frequently encountered in natural symbols, and for once we have a traditional depiction which is not patriarchal or imperial. We have found that a sensitive use of feminine imagery in both artistic representations and texts helps us to amplify and enrich the ways in which we think of God.

And finally — feasting! Whether it is a little roast fish on the beaches of Galilee or the banquet of the Lamb in heaven, the readings of Easter season are full of the joy and satisfaction which Christians share when they dine with Jesus and those who love him. In both our liturgies and our table fellowship we should give back to Easter the real feeling of a FEAST day!

Trinity Sunday

It is worth making a few comments about the origins of this Sunday so that we can see how to adapt it to modern needs. It began in the Middle Ages as a Sunday that marked the conclusion to the liturgical acts and readings by which Christians remembered the life of Christ and the sending of the Holy Spirit on the Sundays and other holy days of Advent through Pentecost. Trinity Sunday was intended to celebrate God in three persons as a sort of theological wrap-up to the great story of salvation which had begun in Advent and concluded in Pentecost. Thomas Beckett was consecrated bishop on Trinity Sunday in 1162, and because he became a very popular saint after his death, this may account for the prominence Trinity Sunday achieved in England as a festival of the church. At any rate the whole Western church was encouraged to observe Trinity Sunday by Pope John XXII in 1334. This has occurred with varying degrees of enthusiasm ever since.

The doctrine of the trinity, by which God is said to exist in three persons and one substance, is a central dogma of Christian theology. The word trinity is not found in the bible, and appears first in A.D. 180. However, from the earliest times Christian thinkers have argued that God appears implicitly in the scriptures as Father, Son, and Holy Spirit, for example in Jesus' teaching in John 14: 11, 16–17 and 26. The doctrine of the trinity has been the subject of debate, defense, refinement, speculation, and adaptation in Christian theology from then until now.

Probably every Christian has been affected by this doctrine. The trinity is contained in the historic creeds which are in use in most churches. With few exceptions every Christian has been baptised "in the name of the Father, Son, and Holy Spirit," although this uniform practice is being challenged by some churches. In prayer, words, art, music, and even the naming of churches, the trinity is omnipresent as the summary of the Christian faith.

But does this summary hold the same power for us today? The trinitarian conception of God has come under attack as being too limiting for defining how God is revealed to the world. By emphasizing the trinity are we neglecting the rich and expansive biblical imagery for God and therefore limiting our own potential religious experience?

Planning

Against this background we met to plan a liturgy for Trinity Sunday. We also had in mind the accumulated heritage of Trinity Sundays we would just as soon forget: the obligatory singing of "Holy, Holy, Holy! Lord God Almighty!"; the valiant attempts by the clergy to explain the trinitarian concept of God within the compass of three points and 25 minutes; the general sense of relief when the service was over. This heritage did not offer much promise for the under-fives, to say nothing of the over-fives, and we didn't think we could pin all our hopes on the device of a clover leaf.

We felt we needed to return to the experiences which precede the intellectual expression of faith, and so we hit upon the idea in this liturgy of calling to mind the experiences by which faith has come alive in us. A popular and appropriate image for the awakening and development of faith is that of the journey. We explored the readings of the day through the prism of the journey, seeking to understand how they might give us insights into our own human journeys to God. In a sense this approach could be used on any Sunday of the year because the whole bible is a record of religious experience, and the excitement of discovering the bible comes from entering the experiences which gave rise to the written words.

To enter symbolically into the theme of journey we decided to hear the three readings "on the move," and to engage the whole congregation in a procession to three places where the readings would occur. Rather than recite a trinitarian creed at a given, static point in the liturgy, we wished to emphasize the dynamic development of faith and so came up with the idea of singing a trinitarian hymn in procession, which would become our statement of faith for the day.

"St. Patrick's Breastplate" is replete with wonderful, strong images for the activity of God in addition to that of the trinity. It also has enough verses for a procession of considerable length. The same rationale led us to delete the sermon in favour of three short dialogues to introduce the readings.

Gathering and Proclamation

People gathered under a large hanging cross in the central space of the church and sang the first two verses of "St. Patrick's Breastplate" (SPB). After the greeting and the collect, the celebrant introduced the theme with reference to a recent movie.

"I wonder how many of you have seen the movie *Stand by Me?* That is a story of four boys going off together on a journey. Through their adventures and all their talking they get to know each other very well. Have any of you been on a journey with your friends or family? (A moderate amount of time was allowed for the sharing of one or two experiences.) That's how Jesus and his friends got to know each other. They travelled around together, talking and eating, listening to Jesus teach and get into arguments, watching him heal sick people. Over three years Jesus and his friends got to know each other very well.

"Today is Trinity Sunday, and we are going to remember today how we get to know Jesus, God, and the Holy Spirit in our own lives.

"As adults it is often useful to think of our lives as a journey in which we are called by God into a relationship with God and others. The maturing process of this relationship is sometimes called faith development, and it happens throughout the course of our lives. Our journey of faith is one way in which we grow and develop.

"To remind ourselves of our own faith journeys we will walk around the church building, making four stops for readings and intercessions. As we walk we will continue to sing 'St. Patrick's Breastplate,' a great statement of faith from the early centuries of the church. This hymn will serve today as our creed.

"At this first stop we will listen to a story about how God was with the Israelites, helping them get out of Egypt and into their own land" (Reading: Deuter-
onomy 4: 32–40).

We then sang two versions of verse 3 (SPB), found in the English and Canadian
hymnals, and processed to the doors at the rear of the church. The second reading was
introduced in the following manner:

"Do you remember what it is like to travel in the car with your family on a long
trip? When we went on our holidays last year there was all sorts of squabbling in the
back seat. (A few experiences were shared, and a few others suppressed by wary
parents.) Squabbling often happens when we travel together. It certainly did with the
disciples. But when we come through these church doors, we remember that it is
Jesus Christ who has called us together to live in peace and be gracious to one another.

"Now we are going to listen to a letter by Paul in which he tries to settle some of
the squabbles of a church and reminds its members of their calling" (Reading:
2 Corinthians 13: 5–14).

During verses 4 and 5 we processed to the font and the congregation was sprinkled with water. The celebrant introduced the gospel.

"Have you ever been going to school and called in at a friend's house on the way?
Sometimes that will happen two or three times, and before you know it there is a
whole gang of you all walking together. (A bit of story-telling from the congregation
ensued.) Another thing about journeys is that on them we gather new friends and
meet new people. That is what happens at baptism. Each time someone is baptised,
they join us on the journey. That is why you were sprinkled with water. It was to
remind you that when you were baptised you were invited to come along with that
great gang of people who follow Jesus.

"Now we are going to listen to the gospel in which Jesus has some things to say
about baptism and also tells us that he will be with us always" (Reading: Matthew 28:
16–20).

Verse 6 of SPB brought the congregation to the pews, while the children gathered
in front of the altar. The celebrant invited the congregation into silent prayer for all
people on their journeys, especially those in need of God's help. The silence lasted
about three minutes and then one of the children led prepared intercessions with a
sung refrain and space for petitions from the congregation. The sharing of the peace
ensued.

Music

In addition to "St. Patrick's Breastplate" other music was chosen to reinforce the journey theme: "The Lord is present in his sanctuary" for the offertory (with rhythm instruments for all the children and any willing adults), and "Lord Jesus, of you I will sing as I journey" after communion.

Dismissal

A rousing adaptation of a Taizé Gloria "Thanks be to God. Alleluia!" repeated several times sent people on their way to the next step on the journey, which for most was breakfast in the church basement.

A Story to Tell

Story-telling as an art is making a comeback. Associations of story-tellers flourish. Writers travel across the country telling their stories in libraries, schools, and community halls. International festivals of story-telling are held in places as different from each other as Toronto and Whitehorse. Aboriginal story-telling is particularly noteworthy: within the aboriginal communities it has been revived as one of the chief means of cultural survival; it has also become a means of communicating aboriginal values to the wider society.

If we were to take a broad view of story-telling and its increased importance in our society, we would include the wrenching public stories told of sexual abuse, of domestic violence, of life in residential schools, of survival of the holocaust....

In an age of sound bites and disconnected bits of information, the story with its classical construction of a beginning, a middle, and an end has a renewed appeal. We are perhaps ready to discover the truths that stories contain, albeit slowly, and are tentatively prepared to invest the time, patience, and attention involved in the act of listening. On the other hand we do need a good story-teller to hold our attention.

As we look at the role of story-telling in the liturgy, there is one central fact to keep in mind: the good story is the one that has meaning to the teller. If a story is being told simply for its effect on the listeners, it will come across as artificial and false. But if the story has in some way spoken to the teller, then it has the potential for speaking to others as well. The meaning of course will never be exactly the same for tellers and listeners; but if there is integrity at the heart of the telling, then the diverse meanings have a deep and strong stream on which to be carried.

Although the bible is often described as the story of God's love for the created order and for a particular people, only a portion of the bible is the result of the art of story-telling and will lend itself to that form of communication today. In addition to finding a good plot and characterization in a biblical passage that can be formed into a story, we should also be alive to the symbols that lie imbedded. Stories often contain symbols of great religious potency that will remain in memory as a focus for meaning long after the plot has vanished.

Much of the advice for public reading of the bible is also applicable to story telling. Rehearsal is essential, and someone with experience in public speaking or acting will be a valuable critic. This person will help make the necessary adjustments for voice modulation, tempo, and acoustics. Can the speaker be seen and heard in the full church building with all of the normal activity and distractions that a large group of people create? Any listener can give valuable feedback in rehearsal about focussing on the essentials of the story, simplicity, and spontaneity. We are not expected to be professionals, but with practice and care we can make a story come alive.

Story-telling in the liturgy is not a performance, but it does make use of narrative and dramatic art. It may be described as the art of sensitively revealing dramatic narrative, characterization, and symbol so that the listeners become participants and discover meaning for their lives in the story. Here are seven examples.

Simple Retelling: The Story of the Blind Man (Luke 18: 35–43)

Within the limitations imposed by many church buildings, the teller creates a relaxed and natural atmosphere, perhaps by gathering a group of children around the place where the story is to be told. The teller may sit down with the children; joining their level creates a sense of equality. However, the questions of visibility and audibility have to be faced. An elevated space and the use of a microphone are possible solutions.

A focussing question may be asked which invites response: "Have you ever thought what it must be like to be blind?" And after the response: "Well, let me tell you a story.... " At this point the story should be told from memory, usually directly from the biblical narrative, which prevents falling into the temptation of adding extraneous, distracting detail. To pick up on the initial focus, the teller then can invite response from any number of points of view: that of the blind man (Shouldn't he have kept quiet?), the disciples (Was it right to protect Jesus from these beggars?), Jesus (Why did he stop?). These responses, when combined with some preparation on the part of the teller which leads the listeners into their own experiences, can normally provide a very engaging dialogue sermon in addition to an enlivened gospel.

Old Testament stories, Jesus' healings, miracle stories, and many of the parables are open to this simple treatment. However, simplicity requires just as much preparation as something more complex! Behind the work of memorization the teller needs to ask, "Why am I telling this story? What meaning does it have for me?"

BIBLICAL DISCOVERY: PAUL AT WORK

Much in the way modern museums try in their displays to take us back in time, biblical characters can be discovered in their context. We can even take this approach one step further by interviewing the character and making connections to the present. Paul may be discovered at his writing desk and then asked a series of questions by an ingenuous interviewer to establish who he is, where and when he is living, who he is writing to and why, all of which lead into a reading of his letter. At the finish, either Paul or members of the congregation could be asked what should be written to the churches on the same theme today. For this approach to be effective it is not necessary to have all the costumes, props, and smells of the first century. All you really need is a table, a piece of paper, a pen (or a computer), and a person who has entered for a short space of time into the character of Paul, although dressed in totally modern clothes. It will of course be quite natural to read from the letter being composed.

BIBLICAL DISCOVERY, WITH STAGE EFFECTS: ISAIAH'S VISION (ISAIAH 2:1–5)

In this variation on the biblical discovery, some of the natural dramatic resources of the church were put to use. People gathered around the altar as they sang the first three verses of "Bright the vision that delighted." Every available container was stoked with burning coals and spoonfuls of incense soon created clouds of smoke which surrounded everyone. Suddenly a white-robed figure with a booming voice emerged and announced, "I am Isaiah the prophet. This is the vision I received from the Lord." He continued with the first three verses of Isaiah 6, the last of which was altered to "They were calling ceaselessly to one another, and singing this hymn of praise," which provided an introduction for the congregation to sing "Lord your glory fills the heaven" again. Isaiah continued to the end of verse eight and with a resounding "Thanks be to God," the congregation completed the hymn as they returned to their seats in the nave of the church. It should be cautioned that verisimilitude sometimes must give way to common sense: Isaiah did not have to endure one of the burning coals being touched to his lips.

Making Connections: The Widow of Nain (Luke 7:11–17)

Sometimes in the lectionary there is the opportunity to make a connection between two readings. How would the characters in a New Testament story have reacted if they had listened to the earlier story from the Old Testament (as they undoubtedly did)? This question can then lead creatively into a challenge to discern the intersections of the biblical stories with our own lives. One Sunday we listened to the story of Elijah and the widow (1 Kings 17:8–24). The gospel was the story of the widow of Nain. Here is how we made the connection:

NARRATOR (discovering and speaking to a young man): You've been in the church. Did you hear the story of Elijah, the widow, and her son?

YOUNG MAN: Yes, I've heard that story of Elijah many times. My mother had a special fondness for it. It seemed to comfort her after my father died, as if to reassure her that God would look after widows.

But, you know, that story happened long ago. People like Elijah don't come along every day. And Elijah, he was one of the greatest of our prophets. Perhaps the greatest. I didn't think there would ever be another like him.

There was something about the way my mother told that story. It was as if she hoped it would keep any further evil away from our house. But in the story the widow's only son falls sick and dies. And what if there is no Elijah to bring him back to life? What then? Does God still care for the widows today?

That's what I remember thinking as I lay sick on my bed, burning with fever, my mother with her hollow eyes staring desperately into my face until I remembered no more.

NARRATOR: Others did remember. We have your story here, in this book. It was told over and over again and became part of the good news of Jesus Christ. (Luke 7: 11–17 is told.)

YOUNG MAN: You probably want to know what it was like being dead. Everyone asks me that. Inquisitive human nature — half-fascinated with death, more than half afraid of it. Well, all I'll say is that I'm not afraid any more. The voice that called me out of my death was stronger than anything I've heard before or since. I didn't think a voice could be stronger than death, but this man's voice was filled with compassion and life. It called me out of a black nothingness into this person you see before you. I look pretty much the same as I did before. Getting older like everyone else. But I'm not afraid of death anymore, or of anything for that matter.

And when my mother and I hear that story of the widow, her son, and Elijah read in the synagogue, we know we have our own story to tell about God's compassion. God has visited his people. That is our good news. (Text by PM.)

An Unlikely Point of View: Elijah and the Widow (1 Kings 17:8–24)

The previous example connected the stories of the two widows through the experience of one of the sons. Sometimes a story can be given new life by telling it from an unusual point of view. The *City of Gold* is a remarkable book in which selected Old Testament stories are told this way. For example, the crossing of the Red Sea is told from the point of view of the Egyptian soldiers. Similar to the example above and with some borrowing from The *City of Gold*, here is a dramatic retelling of the Elijah story. In the background children held vividly coloured strips of cloth of about 3' x 20' and created waves to illustrate the emotions and feelings present in the story.

NARRATOR: It was all a long time ago, but it wasn't. It isn't the sort of thing you forget. But let's start at the beginning. When I was a boy, I lived in Zarephath — perhaps you know it? It's a walled city in Sidon. (Green and blue cloths are waved.) A nice place to grow up, green and lush, fertile country really — until the famine came. (Brown and black cloths are waved.) It started slowly. No rain came. The grass shrivelled. Then all the vegetation began to die. What was once green and growing was now shrivelled and dead. The animals too began to die, and the people.

My mother did the best she could, but even if we'd been rich, there was simply no food to be got. At last, as my mother told the story, even her struggles came to an end.

She went outside the city walls to gather sticks for a last fire for our last meagre meal. (Mother wanders back and forth, bending over to pick up imaginary sticks.)

ELIJAH: Woman of Zarephath, bring a little water, for I am thirsty. And bring me a little morsel of bread in your hand, too.

WIDOW: Stranger, I have nothing in my house but a tiny handful of flour and a few drops of oil at the bottom of the jug. You see these sticks? I'm just gathering them so I may prepare that flour and oil into a small loaf. My son and I will eat it and then we will die.

ELIJAH: Do not be afraid. Go and do just what you say. But, first, bake me a little cake and bring it to me and then go and cook for yourself and your child. For I tell you, my God, the Lord God of Israel, says that flour will not be used up and that oil will not run out, until, once again, God decides that it will rain in this land.

NARRATOR: My mother was a practical woman, not easily persuaded by outlandish promises and talk of a god she'd never heard of. But there was something about that stranger. Anyway, she did what he said — and he was right. That prophet came to live in our house and the famine continued, but somehow that handful of flour was always there and that oil never ran out.

The next bit I don't remember too well, but I got sick. I remember lying there, half in a dream, no longer even able to eat the bread my mother made daily. She fussed and worried over me, of course, but it didn't help. I got worse and, one day, I died. (Black cloth is waved.) I know that sounds odd, in fact, completely unbelievable. But wait, listen. My mother was frantic with grief. She turned on the stranger.

WIDOW: (Red cloth is waved furiously.) What have you done to me, you who claim to be a man of God! I have brought you into my house and fed you and now the old gods are angry with me and my son is dead!

ELIJAH: Give me your son.

NARRATOR: I don't remember this at all of course. But he carried me upstairs to the room he used and he laid me down upon the bed. Downstairs my mother heard him speaking as though at first he was arguing with someone.

ELIJAH: (Red and purple cloths are waved.) Lord, have I not followed your commands? I have come here to Zarephath, just as you told me. Was it not enough, O Lord? Was it not enough, so that now you have slain the son of the woman who helped me?

NARRATOR: My mother heard that last great shout and she crept up the stairs and peered into the room. She saw him stretch himself over my dead body three times, as if he could force his own life into me. And again he cried out.

ELIJAH: O Lord, my God, let this child's soul come into him again.

NARRATOR (the voice of God): (Gold and blue cloths are waved.) And the Lord hearkened to the voice of Elijah. And the soul of the child came into him again. And he revived.

ELIJAH: See! Your son lives!

WIDOW: Now I know that you are a man of God and that the word of the Lord in your mouth is truth. (All cloths are waved for five seconds. Finis. Text by Viola Lang.)

JUMPING INTO THE PRESENT: THE WISE AND FOOLISH MAIDENS (MATTHEW 25: 1–12)

In the previous examples some degree of historical distance was maintained. We know that we are in the present and that the person representing Elijah, Paul, or the widow's son exists in the past. Even though we are allowed to transgress the time barrier, the effect conveyed by the story relies upon the distance between the present and the past. This effect would be destroyed if, for example, Paul were to step out of character and suddenly address the congregation in his role as treasurer of the parish.

Historical distance does require some minimal sophistication. We seek to understand what happened in the past in order to see the present with new eyes. In some cases the same purpose can be served by making the transition from past to present within the presentation itself, so that the biblical story is told as if it was happening today. The next example takes one of Jesus' parables and recasts it into present-day terms, involving the children of the congregation in the process.

The story-teller gathered all the children at the front of the church and asked if anyone had ever been late for anything. What did it feel like? Did they prefer being on time? After a few responses she said that Jesus told a story about being late and being ready, and that everyone could have a part in it. The scene was a wedding party at night with guests waiting for the bride and groom to come. A bride and groom with family attendants were chosen, given suitable hats, and sent to the back of the church. The others were ushers and bridesmaids who were given flashlights and remained at the front. Half of this group were given spare batteries.

The story-teller began the parable, making the appropriate modern interpolations. The ushers and bridesmaids laid down to sleep, but then were awakened by a great shout from the back of the church, "The bride and groom are coming!" The narrator continued: "Everyone got up, but because it was late, most of the batteries had run out. (The flashlights were dead!) Only some had thought to bring extra batteries. The others wanted them to share, but there weren't enough to go around. They rushed off to try to buy some more. (A desperate rush to the all-night corner store in the church basement.) But while they were gone the families arrived and the party began. (Arrival of the bride and groom with attendants.) And when the ushers and bridesmaids who weren't prepared got back, the door to the party was shut and it was too late for them to get in." (Return of the unprepared ushers and bridesmaids.)

This participatory parable gave rise to enthusiastic debriefing about being ready or being unprepared, and the homily was built on these comments. The logistics had to be carefully thought through, a few props procured, and rather a lot of flashlights and batteries collected. However, there was no rehearsal necessary, as the children were able to take on roles within the story with a minimal amount of instruction which did not distract from the narrative. Similar examples of this technique can be found in the Passion Sunday, Good Friday, and Easter liturgies.

A Dramatic Dialogue: Jesus and Nicodemus (John 3:1–17)

In case there is some suspicion that the advice given at the beginning of this section on simplicity has been gradually eroded, we shall end with a New Testament passage that is easily divided into speaking parts. There are a number of dialogues in the fourth gospel which lend themselves to this technique because they have dramatic movement and revelation of character. Many other passages which have dialogue in them turn out on closer inspection to be unsuitable for dramatic presentation, because the dynamic between the speakers is not really conveyed by the dialogue itself.

In the encounter between Jesus and Nicodemus, the narrator creates a bridge between the congregation and the conversation, allowing them to listen in, as it were, with the introduction ..."Now there was a man of the Pharisees," and commenting on its significance with the concluding remarks "For God so loved the world." Jesus and Nicodemus engage in debate without any interruptions from the narrator. These parts can be memorized or read from a script. In either case rehearsal is important to bring out the characterization and the dynamic energy of the dialogue. The choice of readers can also hint at levels of meaning: Nicodemus was once played by an educational consultant and his challenger was a young school girl. "How can this be? You, a teacher of Israel, and you don't understand?"

FINAL CAVEATS

If any of these story-telling and dramatic techniques are to enhance communication of God's word, they must be chosen carefully. Carefully means seeking to understand the meaning of the biblical story and having the method of presentation grow out of this search.

As with reading, preparation and rehearsal are essential. Stories do not tell themselves. The work of rehearsal is often the means for the story to enter the soul of the teller.

Often a simple detail is all that is required to bring a story to life. A mother sat on a rocking chair on the chancel steps, gathered children around her, and began, "My little children, I am writing this to you so that you may not sin..." (1 John 2).

There will probably be more acceptance of experiments with story-telling and drama if they are not tried frequently and if reading is retained as the normal mode of presentation.

Parish Days

These liturgies have come from experiences in Ottawa, Toronto, and Wernigerode, Germany. What they have in common is that they all encompassed a good part of the weekend, all day Saturday or a Saturday flowing into Sunday. They also occurred in parishes, or in the case of Toronto, a group of parishes, which had more than 150 regular worshippers. These liturgies came from larger churches which have considerable resources at their disposal. Churches with fewer members could certainly manage similar programs and liturgies, but would probably need to scale down the level of activity.

Many German Lutheran churches have the custom of holding a parish day on or near their patronal festival. The animating philosophy behind the parish day I attended was to build community in an alienating society that was driven towards achievement. The society of what was then East Germany had a very high divorce rate, a very low birth rate, and little regard for children. People had no time for leisure, and even the leisure they had was taken up with highly competitive sports and other activities. Although the church had come to terms with living in a socialist country, the church leaders decided that the constant drive for higher achievement was spiritually and morally corrosive. In opposition to what they saw happening in the society around them they decided to encourage the concepts of the church as a family and the church as a place of play and recreation.

The church was to be a place where all generations could talk, play, learn, and pray together. Adults with no children would have the opportunity to relate to children, and similarly children who had been abandoned by their parents would find in the church family adults who cared about them. Furthermore, amidst the high seriousness of a socialist state, the church proclaimed that the gospel is fun. It shouldn't be imagined that these ideas were universally acclaimed by all the congregations. Most protestant denominations have in their heritage a measure of sobriety and German Lutherans are not exempt. However, the parish day was one place where some congregations found an opportunity for putting "the gospel is fun" into practice.

The parish day I attended began in the early afternoon inside the medieval church building with a welcome and a funny story by the pastor. A saturnine group of brass musicians provided some lugubrious and unpromising entertainment, but then things brightened up with a sprightly young woman who led us singing out to the parish hall for cakes and coffee. Afterwards, games for the children and painted faces, all done in orderly Germanic fashion. Then into the church for a short concert with recorder and organ. Then back to the hall for a spirited dramatized version of Snow White with many contemporary references to the local mines. Next, ice cream; then into the church for a concert of Bach and Beatles by a very accomplished choir. A curious supper was served of various lardy spreads, pickles, and beer. We next had a simple service with prayer for community life. Finally we gathered outside around a bonfire to join in some vigorous dances and jolly songs. Story-telling, talking, then we all went home. Children and adults of all ages, singles, couples, local orphans, lovers, Christians, and agnostics, and who knows who else, had been together for 10 hours. It was one of the few opportunities they had for relaxing together. Although the day wasn't overtly religious, at its heart was the conviction that the gospel is humane and counter-cultural: people matter, community matters.

The Germans are not alone in the need to humanize a stressful existence and affirm the value of building a diverse and inclusive community. Canada is one of the most urbanized countries in the world, and with urbanization come many of the forces that turn us into isolated individuals without a natural community to which we belong. The two Canadian parishes who have contributed these next programs and liturgies were aware of the alienating conditions of their social context as they did their planning, and although the Saturday events had a definite educational focus, they were relaxed enough to allow for lots of human interaction amongst the generations. In both cases the Saturday program was planned to lead into Sunday liturgy, with the result that the worship had lots of participation and energy.

You may pick up ideas which you wish to try from the descriptions which follow. Most of all these accounts should be seen as an encouragement to be radically counter-cultural in your own way and live out the gospel by having fun.

God's Creation and Us

This learning and liturgical event was planned as a three-hour workshop on Saturday to be followed the next day by a eucharist which would pick up the themes of the workshop. The purpose was to explore ways in which Christians could respond to the environmental crisis. The Sunday was the first Sunday in Lent. The planners and participants were drawn from the Anglican churches in the Parkdale deanery, which is in downtown Toronto. The planning team included older children, teenagers, parents, clergy, and adults with experience in education and social justice.

THE SATURDAY EVENT

ARRIVALS

As people came in they were invited to make name tags for themselves. They were asked to write down something they loved about the earth on a paper flower and something they could do to care for creation on a raindrop. The flowers and rain drops were pinned to a mural which became a visual focus for the day. A bowling game with old milk bottles and water play with detergent bottles engaged the younger children.

INTRODUCTION

Participants were asked to introduce themselves to two previously unknown people of different ages. The session began with a slide show of Canadian wilderness scenes accompanied by a reading of the creation story. People were then asked to join one of four workshops.

WORKSHOPS

Trees: This workshop was led by two older children who explained the function of forests in the ecosystem and why the world's forests are in danger. Ideas for preserving forests were written on large leaves and pasted to a bare tree made from a cardboard box.

Water: Participants decorated cardboard fish with words and symbols to show the value of the gift of water. Similarly, dragons were festooned with words and symbols showing the sources of waste and pollution. Next there was a discussion about ideas for positive action, both in changing personal lifestyles and in lobbying government and industry. These ideas were written on raindrops. Fish, dragons, and raindrops were placed on a sea mural, and people moved on to other activities such as letter writing, organizing a petition, and creating posters. A water table replete with aquatic creatures proved very popular with the young children. Finally, everyone was invited to drink a glass of water and pay what they thought it was worth, the proceeds going to local and international environmental agencies.

Air: A multitude of resource materials was on hand for adults and teenagers to read and learn about the sources of air pollution. The children bowled down aerosol cans. Everyone tried the science experiment in which melted snow and tap water were tested for acidity using litmus paper. Posters were created and letters of protest written.

Recycling: Everyone formed a circle to represent the earth. Nothing could enter it or leave it. In the centre was a pile of garbage composed of household items. Some of the garbage would have to be thrown away, some should never have been bought in the first place, and the rest could be composted, recycled, or reused. Then a gift-wrapped package with a tag "To humanity from God" was opened, and revealed a variety of natural treasures which were discussed. These were compared with a can of potatoes: although God's gifts, such as potatoes, are all recyclable, we often turn them into garbage problems.

Each member became a garbage consultant, picking up an object from the garbage pile and explaining what could be done with it. Other ideas for preserving the environment were shared. To put learning into practice participants made bird-feeders out of cast-off articles or created signs for church halls and kitchens to remind their users of environmentally friendly practices.

An impromptu addition to the recycling centre was an enormous cardboard box which was salvaged from the garbage. Armed with scissors, paints, markers, and masking tape, a team of builders transformed the carton into an elaborate playhouse/fortress (depending upon one's point of view), complete with shutters and basketball hoop. This was truly an intergenerational effort: workers ranged from preschoolers to seniors and included an architect.

An ecologically sound and nutritious lunch was served, the workshops were repeated, and the Saturday event was closed with a short act of prayer, praise, and commitment.

The Sunday Liturgy

Saturday had focussed concerns about the environment and given expression to these concerns through a variety of creative activities. The purpose of the Sunday liturgy was to lift up these concerns in the context of worship, and to turn the activities of learning and community creation into an act of prayer. However, many of the people who came to worship on Sunday morning had not been present on Saturday, and so the liturgy had to be designed to include them as well.

This liturgy is noteworthy for its use of creative materials, most of which were the products of the previous day's activities. However, the creativity didn't stop with art work, because some of the hymns and all of the litanies were written by members of the congregation to express the environmental theme.

Gathering of the Community

People gathered in the centre of the church while a simple Kyrie was sung over and over to create a sombre atmosphere. The greeting was exchanged and a short introduction to the liturgy was given, followed by the collect for the first Sunday in Lent (which is happily appropriate to the theme).

A Procession of Penitence

The Old Testament reading of Genesis 2:4b–9, 15–17, 25–3:7 was read, and then the whole congregation processed to three stations: the breath of life (near the church entrance), the water of life (at the font), and the tree of life (under a cross). Each station had a strong visual focus which used the materials from the Saturday work shop. At each station a brief description of the Saturday workshop was given with an emphasis on the responsibility of Christians to care for God's creation. Then a two-part litany was prayed: petitions of repentance, acknowledging our complicity in the environmental crisis, and petitions for renewal and safety of all living things. This pattern of description and two-part litany was repeated at each station. A simple hymn composed for the occasion was sung to the tune "We shall overcome," as the congregation moved from station to station.

At each station children picked up images of the creation appropriate to the station. The last station was positioned close to the altar, and during the singing of the Kyrie they pasted these images on a partially constructed altar frontal to make a renewed garden.

On the way to the breath of life:

We have lost our way, we have lost our way, we have lost our way today. But deep in my heart I do believe that God will show the way today.

We destroy God's world.... But deep in my heart I do believe that God will save the world today.

We are formed of dust.... But deep in my heart I do believe that God will breathe in us today.

On the way to the water of life:

We are still afraid.... But deep in my heart I do believe that God will give us strength today.

The waters bring no life.... But deep in my heart I do believe that God can quench Earth's thirst today.

On the way to the tree of life:

We still turn away.... But deep in my heart I do believe that God will turn us back today.

The world cries out in pain.... But deep in my heart I do believe that God will heal the world today.

The litanies of penitence were brought to a conclusion by the singing of the original Kyrie, this time with verses added. An absolution was given.

The Proclamation of the Word

The New Testament readings for this Sunday were Romans 5:12–19 and Matthew 4:1–11. The intention was to create a more positive, hopeful atmosphere at this point, and so a hymn written by St. Patrick abounding in natural imagery was sung to the tune "Morning has broken."

A dialogue sermon tied the events of Saturday with the Sunday liturgy. The children were asked what they had enjoyed most during the workshop on the previous day. Their attention was drawn to the way in which the creations and activities of Saturday had formed the first part of Sunday's service. What did they think of praying for the trees, for clean water, for recycling? Then, using the example of the recycled cardboard box, the sermon emphasized the value of play and creativity as ways of appreciating the wonder of God's creation. Appreciation lies at the heart of our desire and ability to care for creation.

The Apostles' Creed, set in question and response form, was used with the following additions:

CELEBRANT: Will you be responsible in your use of the created order and modest in your consumption of non-renewable resources?

PEOPLE: We will with God's help.

CELEBRANT: Will you seek to protect and preserve the environment from human greed and carelessness?

PEOPLE: We will with God's help.

The peace followed directly. The offering of home-baked bread and wine was brought up to a hymn composed by a member of the congregation. A eucharistic prayer, emphasizing the created order, was sung with Taizé responses throughout. After communion "Let all things now living" was sung and then a silent space was created for people to offer their spontaneous prayers of petition and thanksgiving. Following the blessing and dismissal, people were invited to select cards on which were printed household hints for environmental protection, so that the dismissal "to love and serve the Lord" could be given a practical point of reference. The food and drink at the coffee hour were more nutritional than is usually the case, and posters created the day before decorated the gathering space. Styrofoam cups were quickly replaced with washable china.

Hymn for the preparation of the gifts written by Brenda Stringer (may be reprinted for parish use only). Tune: Kingsfold.

1. Creator of the Earth and Heavens,
You sent your only Son
To live and die as one of us
That your will might be done:
Teach us to recognize our Lord
In every human face,
And in all living things to own
The spirit of your grace

2. Your power made all living things
To blossom from the dust.
You made this fruitful Earth our home,
A garden in our trust.
Lord teach us reverence for the life
Committed to our care,
Preserving all your precious gifts
In water, earth and air.

3. You gave us forests proud and deep.
    You gave us fertile land.
    Our axe and plough turn
     both to dust,
    Vast fields of blowing sand.
    The rivers that once teemed with fish
    Now burn with poisoned rain.
    The land is sown with seeds of death:
    Lord, make us turn again.

4. God make us recognize at last
    How fragile is this land.
    Let not the creatures you gave breath
    Die at their keepers' hand.
    Teach us to choose the way of life
    Above the way of gain,
    That Earth restored may
    praise its Lord
    And the desert bloom again.

An evaluation of the weekend was that the experience was rich in commitment, celebration, and learning. Children and young people took an active leadership role. Intergenerational events attract not only families with children and teenagers, but also single people and older people who like to be part of a varied community. Planning and decision making that includes children and young people takes longer but reaps greater rewards.

Surprise, Amazement, and Hope

This weekend event is described as an example of liturgical planning emerging from a day-long intergenerational meditation upon Isaiah 49: 1–13. The details of the Saturday workshop and the Sunday liturgy are not included, but the general description should serve as a guide for parishes that wish to find meaning and inspiration in the biblical record for their corporate life.

A large urban congregation was experiencing unease. A formerly large Sunday school had decreased in numbers and the youth program was going through a change. There was a sense of crisis over the increasing lack of involvement of young people in ministry and worship. Many of the adult leaders were committed to the classroom model of teaching, but had been creatively disturbed by some new ideas about the way in which faith is learned and were wondering how these ideas could be successfully integrated into a fairly rigid Sunday pattern of liturgy and structured learning. Could the old days of large, successful Christian education programming in which all ages were separated from each other and in which children and young people learned while adults worshipped be brought back? Or was it necessary to rethink how we discovered faith?

A group from the parish wrestled with these questions and decided to engage in an experiment in which, over a weekend, all ages would learn from and with each other, and all would worship together. Appropriately, the first reading appointed for the Sunday liturgy was Isaiah 49: 1–13, in which the prophet speaks of both the experience of despondency and the exalted vision of Israel's mission. When these two are contrasted the result is surprise, amazement, and hope: surprise that there is anything more to be said after reiterating the conditions of Israel's defeat; amazement that Israel's mission is far more than returning to the happy conditions of the old days; hope that the vision can be realized. As the parish group reflected on this passage, they came to see that these were words for their own congregational life and a call to try a radical new way.

They proposed a weekend workshop which would explore a new way of discovering the faith, in which all participants would be teachers and all would be learners together. A team of workshop leaders was drawn together to explain the concept. They engaged in a study of the passage and were encouraged to think of how the theme of surprise, amazement, and hope could be explored in creative activities that would appeal to all ages. Leaders, both teenagers and adults, emerged who were willing to lead sessions in movement, visual arts, creative writing, drama, music, games, and critical thinking. The second part of the workshop would be devoted to planning the Sunday liturgy.

The Saturday workshop began with music and community-building activities in which all could participate. Two stories were told about surprises: one for young children about receiving an unexpected gift from Santa Claus, and the other for teenagers about the unexpected benefits of going on an extended educational exchange. Everyone was invited to think of a surprise they had experienced and then to express that surprise by shaping a piece of clay and talking to their neighbour. (Some of the shapes were surprises in themselves.)

Then the story of the Isaiah passage was told in a simple fashion: "The people of Israel were taken into exile and felt that God had deserted them. After 50 years there was no cause for celebration; there were few births and no singing. Then an amazing thing happened. God spoke through a prophet and said that they would be led back to Jerusalem. They would have children, food, and singing, because God is stronger than the armies that captured them. This was quite a surprise."

Leaders then gave a brief description of their workshops and everyone was free to choose which one they wanted to go into. A space to escape was created as an over-flow for those who lost interest in the activity and needed an alternative. Co-operative games and music provided a gathering opportunity for all participants before sharing a meal together.

Following the meal a transition was made to liturgical planning. Not every liturgy has the benefit of 50 planners. On the other hand, not every liturgy is put together the day before.

Everyone had had an enjoyable morning exploring surprises in their lives through various media. There had also been some corporate surprise in that it was possible to enter into a mode of learning different from the traditional teacher-student relation-ship. Now the question was "How can we celebrate the surprises of God in our lives tomorrow?"

The basic structure of the eucharist was retained. People were invited to think about how the various creative activities in which they had engaged could be used to bring to life each liturgical part: the physical arrangement of the building and its decoration; the act of welcoming as people arrived; the greeting and gathering of the community; the liturgy of the word; the prayers of the people, confession, absolution and peace; the offering of symbols of ourselves; the great thanksgiving; the act of receiving; an expression of hospitality after the dismissal. All these and other aspects were considered and then groups formed to plan one particular part of the liturgy. Wonderful visual creations emerged; stories were composed; a dance at the offertory was choreographed; music written and chosen, intercessions made, a fresh exchange of the peace devised.

There were some anxious moments in the course of this planning. Could all the creativity be brought into coherence? Could this diverse community be trusted to plan and implement a liturgy in a parish used to having this done by professionals?

The vitality and energy of the liturgy took everyone by surprise, both the planners and the people who congregated to worship that Sunday morning. It was an illustra-tion of Joseph Gelineau's distinction between congregation and community. The community plans the liturgy for the congregation. In this case a new community was created on Saturday morning and out of that experience an energetic expression of praise was developed which drew into its orbit the many other disparate individuals who made up the Sunday congregation.

Intercessory Prayer

"Intercession at its best is our affirming the good purposes of God in the whole universe, even if they cannot be fathomed," writes Robin Green in *Only Connect* (p. 43). This comment alludes to at least three important aspects of intercessory prayer: we pray with confidence and hope; we bring the whole world into our view (but not all at once); we remain in an attitude of awe and dependence before the mystery of God. The intercessions and the confession can be one of the most powerful parts of the liturgy because they are the intersection between the deepest concerns of humanity and the present, creative, and redeeming work of God.

How is this intersection achieved? We have all participated in both good and bad intercessions and will have our particular reasons for distinguishing between the two. Is it a matter of preparation? Yes, but once the prepared intercessions did not arrive and so the congregation prayed for what was on their hearts and minds. Is it a matter of spontaneity? Yes, but once spontaneous prayer allowed one person to dominate the intercessions with his obsessions. Is it a matter of authenticity and integrity? Yes.

Without being prescriptive and allowing for exceptions, we can venture a few guidelines for intercessory prayer:

— The intercessions are called the prayers of the people for a good reason. They are a yearning for God's presence in the life of the world, and so they are most suitably expressed by people whose vocation is in the world.

— Intercessions require preparation, and space should be given for others to add their prayers.

— Prayer of any sort is directed to God and is therefore different from a sermon which is directed to people. Sometimes people need help in discerning the difference.

— If in doubt, short, direct prayer is best. God is normally well informed on most subjects and doesn't need a lot of detail or instruction.

— Intercessions are the prayers of the people and not of an individual person. The intercessor is praying on behalf of all those present and therefore should attempt to offer prayer that everyone can enter into.

— Jesus taught that prayer should be insistent. Nowhere did he say it should be polite.

— The renewal movement has recaptured the sense of the presence of God in Christian individuals and groups. This sense needs to be balanced by an appreciation for God's action in the whole world.

— We always pray with awe, wonder, and dependence upon God's grace.

For those planning a liturgy the intercessions usually involve choosing people to prepare them and creating an atmosphere in which the whole congregation can enter into prayer.

Who do we ask to pray? Although some people do have a special gift for composing intercessions that awaken us to the need of humanity for God, we can also look to people who may not have skill with words but who bring the power of experience and empathy. A nurse may be the best person to pray for the sick, an unemployed person for those suffering from economic deprivation, a refugee for those displaced from their country, and so on. If there is a particular focus to the liturgy, such as God's care for the poor, then this can be carried through in the intercessions by finding people from the congregation who identify with the focus and are prepared to give it particular expression in prayer. Alternatively, sometimes the starting point is the experience of someone who has been healed or reconciled or had a life-changing encounter. This person may be able to pray on behalf of the whole congregation with a lively sense of God's transforming power.

Intercessions can be prepared by individuals or by groups, such as family members. A parent and child will bring the perspectives of two generations, and their leadership will allow several age groups to identify with them. Sophia Cavalletti in *The Religious Potential of the Child* remarks that children's prayer is expressed in short and essential phrases, ideal for communal intercessions. They may lack sophistication, but they do bring a refreshing directness. On one occasion the theme of the liturgy was God's care for the children of the world, and a group of parish children led the intercessions, each child praying for the children of one region of the world.

How do we create a prayerful atmosphere so that people can enter into the action of intercession? Here are four ideas that have been tried with some success: silence, action, symbols, and music.

If used with sensitivity, silence is a great aid to prayer. It is, however, not enough to ask people to be silent and to pray. In corporate prayer (as opposed to individual prayer) we should have a focus, and this can be given verbally or through a visual image. Contrary to popular opinion, young children of three years old and up can remain in silent prayer for several minutes, if they have someone or something to hold in their minds which is concrete and arouses their interest. The focus may be something as simple as, "Let us pray in our hearts for children." All of us, children and adults alike, need to be in a comfortable position in order to remain still and silent even for short periods of time. Also, an imposed silence which is not entered into by the congregation becomes a controlling mechanism and not an aid to prayer.

I remember a comment from a Quaker friend on silence in worship: "For us 15 minutes is a mere pause." For some congregations 15 seconds produces restlessness, and so silence needs to be introduced and taught as a way of entering into the mystery of God's presence. The moment of restlessness, which can easily be felt in a congregation, is a crisis point in the space created by the silence, but once past the crisis the silence becomes more and more powerful. People can be taught to live through this uncomfortable moment in order to be attentive to God.

Those of us from Western cultures are slowly learning from our more expressive brothers and sisters that it is possible to pray by moving our bodies. It will be a while before our intercessions take on the rhythm of an African dance, but in the meantime we can take some tentative steps away from our confining pews. As intercessions are made candles can be lit, seeds placed in earth, incense sprinkled on coals, or any other number of physical actions carried out that allow us to do something which concretely expresses our inner prayer.

Similar to actions, objects can be used symbolically to focus our minds in prayer. Carefully chosen slides can provide an imaginative counterpoint to the spoken prayers, or they can be used on their own, allowing each person to pray in their hearts from the associations which are conjured up. Large coloured cloths which were used in the liturgy of the word to symbolize strong emotions can be draped over the altar during intercessory prayer, making a link between the two parts of the liturgy. Objects representing each petition can be placed in view, one at a time, for all to see, giving the prayers a reality they sometimes lack.

The chief benefits of using music as a responsive refrain for intercessions are that it allows people the time to pray and it sets a tone or mood for prayer. A repeated sung refrain takes longer than a said response and gives the opportunity for expressing more of ourselves; on the other hand, it also runs the risk of becoming repetitive and boring if it runs beyond the patience of the congregation or is musically trite. Intercessions will have different tones of joy, urgency, sadness, and contrition, often determined by the season. The use of music can enhance these moods. Many churches have discovered that the music of Taizé is well suited to intercessory response, having both a meditative quality and variety in instrumentation. It is music that has grown out of long experience with intercession for reconciliation and peace in the world, and is a gift to the wider church.

A New Song

Jesus sang.

It is rather a puzzle in modern biblical interpretation that so few commentators have seriously tried to recover the musical Jesus for us. And musical he was: he sang when he read the prophecy of Isaiah in the synagogue, he sang the blessing of the bread and cup, he sang the great Hallelujah which closed his last supper, and he sang the psalms to himself on the cross.

If this perspective is a surprise, it is because we have lost the musical roots of our liturgy. Music must have been an integral part of the relationship he had with the Father. We can expect no less in our liturgical music. And yet we seem caught in a society in which there is a great deal of music but very little music-making.

In order to recover some of the authentic traditions of Christian music, we may have to look at the way in which music functions in contemporary non-technological, pre-literate cultures. Ethno-musicologists have long recognized that non-Western musical traditions have much to tell us about the background from which our own music developed. If we can lay aside our notions of "primitive" music for a moment, we can see a few principles which could be of great importance to the church.

Music is communal. Everyone performs. The community, village, or family defines itself through its corporate music-making. It is always inclusive.

Music is vocal. The human voice is the primary instrument. All other wind, string, and percussion instruments are embellishments and additions to the sound of voices.

The leaders of music enable and enhance the communal experience. Every culture has musicians whose talents are recognized and treasured. The leaders have two roles: first, to excite and inspire the community to perform; and second, to embellish and improvise according to their particular gifts.

Music is passed on in an oral tradition. The musical experience is conveyed from generation to generation through communal performance. The music itself changes and develops in new directions. The community is the composer.

Music is spiritual. Music is a gateway to the sacred. The community experiences the transcendence and harmoniousness of the divine in a unique way through music. Worship is impossible without music.

Although we must apologize for such sweeping generalizations, we can see what challenges these principles represent for the development of a renewed liturgical music. In fact, most of these principles are guaranteed to provoke heated discussion in a congregation. Rather than indulge in the predictable polemics which blaze up whenever church music is discussed, we may find it more profitable to look at the planning process and see how the above principles might influence the building of the liturgy.

A little fantasy might help.

Imagine for a moment that you have come to a service in church and find yourself alone in the building — completely alone. Most of us would put on our coats and go home, convinced that a liturgy was impossible. Imagine then that you *do* take off your coat and sit down. If you're all alone, why not sing something? You begin to hum a short melody. You can't think of a text, so you just add some familiar words that are often repeated:

Someone else comes in. Intrigued by the sound, the newcomer sits down and gradually joins you, singing the same repeated melody. A teenager who sings in a rock band arrives and improvises a little two-part harmony.

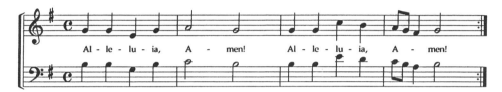

A public school music teacher adds an alto line and her husband hums a simple bass. You have four parts around your melody now.

People are trickling into the church. Some join in the melody because it's so easy to learn. Others lean over the pew, hum along with the other parts, and then lean back to teach them to someone else.

The choir members have found their places in the chancel. They enjoy the complex sound of voices and add a whole series of splendid harmonies.

The junior choir members have clattered in, listened, and put their independently minded heads together. They're not going to be left out: they sing your melody as a round as well.

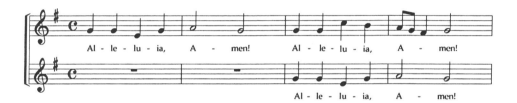

The soprano soloist sings with the choir for a while and then sails off into an improvised descant of truly operatic proportions.

The organist is finally taking off his coat. He sits at the organ, finding the melody under his fingers. His training has always encouraged improvisation, so he adds a new sound and weight to the singing.

The church is nearly full when a ten-year-old flute student arrives with her teacher after her lesson. Taking out her instrument, she can just manage a simple counter melody to the singing. The whole colour of the music changes.

The teacher can't resist either: she gets out her flute, and soon the silver shine of her notes is carrying above the whole assembly.

Finally, the choir director raises his baton, and an ensemble of trumpets, horns, and trombones bring the music to a close.

The community has gathered — the liturgy has begun.

The situation is admittedly fanciful, and the depiction of community co-operation more or less wishful thinking. However, each reader will recognize something in that day-dream which captures a past moment when it could be said that music was the catalyst for a powerful experience of worship.

But is it *good* music?

This writer wrote each line of music as he wrote the story. The melody is a tune that anyone could make up. The people's harmony is such that a church congregation could sing with a bit of help. The choir parts are music that a church choir would have to rehearse before it was performed. The instrumental and organ parts would require technique and attention. So everyone has music that both respected and challenged their abilities.

But is it *good* music?

Well, it's not the "Hallelujah Chorus" — certainly not with those consecutive fifths! It's unlikely to be sung in 50 years' time, or even in 50 days' time.

Then is it good *liturgical* music?

Yes. Although its chances for historic greatness are slim indeed, it met the needs of a particular, albeit imaginary, congregation. And now we can apply those seemingly impossible principles discussed above. The music was communal and accessible to all — no one was excluded. Even a three-year-old child or a blind senior could have joined in because the music was transmitted by example and repetition. The choir and soloist's contributions were not just optional additions: their talents made the familiar into something constantly new. At that point it was only the human voice which could be heard. The organ and instruments brought new colours and new rhythms, but they never took the music away from the people. What we can't know in this little fantasy is what the community said to God and if a voice of unity and love spoke to them in their common prayer.

And yet this piece will probably be "throwaway" music. We will not use it again because it has served a particular liturgy, a particular liturgy which will not occur again. But if we did use it again, it could be used at both a prayer-group meeting in someone's home, and a diocesan service with hundreds of musicians: each liturgy would have different needs and different resources. Musicians looking at this music will see that certain forms — chorale, ostinato, canon, variations, free counterpoint —

seem to lend themselves to a musical expression of our liturgical principles. The musical cell is small and therefore infinitely flexible (the similarity to modern minimalist technique is not accidental). Note, however, that the available resources dictated the shape of the music. If all a church could muster was the 10-year-old flautist and a pianist, the music would be as satisfactory as if a professional choir and orchestra performed it in a great cathedral.

It should be pointed out that we are advocating a new perspective to liturgical music, not a particular style. Although modern criticism tends to focus on the use of cathedral and "art" music in the liturgy, nearly all popular styles of sacred music are equally performer-oriented and presume a passive observer congregation. Most rock and popular styles are not participatory. In an ideal situation, we would have the freedom to access and use all repertoires, be they "serious" or "throwaway."

Our fantasy liturgy should also give us our first step in planning music in the liturgy: we must know the talents of our community. In most parishes that means looking further than the "musical establishment" represented by the organist and the choir. In many churches, choirs and organists have worked for so long with unrealistic models that morale and musicality have plummeted. Why should a parish lament for even a moment that their music does not sound like King's College, Cambridge, when the latter has a musical budget equal to the total budgets of a hundred parishes? Nor should we restrict our sounds to merely the choir and organ. Instruments have a long and distinguished history in the Western church. And in non-Western churches, we can find a wide variety of percussion instruments. The old model is destructive: pass on to something else which builds up the community.

Every church needs a musical talent inventory. Who can sing? Classical music? Popular music? Every week? Once a month? Who can play the piano? The synthesizer? The guitar? Who can play an instrument? Who can but hasn't played for years? Who has a daughter, a brother, or a friend who plays an instrument in school?

If the right questions are asked and the model is kept broad and inclusive, the names will appear. Not all of them need to be asked at once. Start with a small core group which can expand or contract as talent is needed or becomes available. Just as you have to walk through the church building to visualize what a liturgy will look like, you have to know your resources before you can *hear* what the liturgy will sound like.

When the planning group meets, it should extend that imaginary hearing to its discussion. As the group works through the readings and themes, texts will begin to suggest themselves. That is straightforward because it is still a literary task, and most planners still think in terms of words rather than their expression. It may be worthwhile, therefore, to listen to some of the essential moments in the eucharist.

Our imaginary liturgy allowed a community to define its unity and diversity through a gradual evolution and development of the music. That kind of experience is valuable when the themes of the liturgy seem to ask for a measure of reflection or a strong corporate bond. At other times the music for the gathering of the community may accompany physical movement: a procession or a dance. A wholly different character may be needed if a quiet introspective mood is required. In each case, the music must lead the worshipper into the celebration.

A scriptural reading in any liturgy is the first statement of a dialogue. We cannot pass on to another reading until we have made an appropriate response. Historically, music has always been the medium through which we answer the voice of God speaking to us in scripture. Thus, we have to stop and feel what the response should be. What is the emotion of our answer? The psalms have always been a rich source of responses: they are musical texts of incomparable beauty. Another musical form which is a valuable structure is the respond, in which the verses of the psalms sung by a soloist are successively acclaimed with a refrain. For instance, we could use that "Alleluia! Amen!" melody after verses sung over the same harmonies.

Sing to the Lord a new song; sing to the Lord, all the whole earth.

Each time that the refrain returned, we would hear a new colour or sonority, as the choir, soloists, and instrumentalists introduced new variations on the congregation's response.

On some occasions, the music will blossom inside the reading itself: Ruth's words to Naomi, Mary's canticle of praise, the song of the angels to the shepherds, the heavenly music to the Lamb. All of these texts have such resonance and beauty that singing them gives a compelling power which prosaically disappears when they are merely spoken. Many readings themselves were originally songs: the opening of John's gospel, the song of Miriam at the Exodus, the hymns in the epistles to the Ephesians and Philippians. All of these gain in strength when their music is restored.

Nor should we forget the most powerful musical response of all: silence. Considered, measured silence before or during the prayers of the people is an important musical statement. The prayers also gain in breadth and weight when the corporate response is sung. Even a short repeated phrase such as "Lord have mercy" grows in urgency as it is repeated with vocal and instrumental variations.

Perhaps the greatest musical challenge is the eucharistic prayer. In most modern rites, the prayer of consecration of the bread and wine is supported by the participation of the whole community. As the celebrant sings the history of salvation and asks for the saving grace of God, the people lend their prayer and assent in acclamations such as "Glory to you for ever." At this central moment, we need the fullest participation of the people. A simple adaptation of our refrain gives us an acclamation which hardly needs to be learned. Our eyes and minds remain focussed on the action taking place.

The musical forms which we outlined above allow us great opportunities to develop music which we can really use to pray and respond to God. It is precisely because a community's prayer and thanksgiving are so important that we must encourage our churches to write and produce their own music. Many parish musicians are paralysed by the fear that someone is going to judge their compositions. If the liturgical principles above are our criteria for success, then the inhibitions will disappear and churches will begin to develop their own musical language. The musical examples reproduced in this chapter are not great music, judged by the compositional standards of either contemporary classical music or current popular traditions. They may not be great, but they are useful. When we create our own liturgical music, we animate and illuminate our worship with an inner spirit which the whole community shares.

A Note about Sources

Although there are many places to which we can turn for resources and reflection about music in liturgy, we might add that our particular approach has been heavily influenced by a number of centres.

1) The music of the Taizé community in France has been an ongoing experiment under the direction of Jacques Berthier. The project has tried to develop a musical style which will draw its participants into prayer. This is a special challenge as the worshippers at Taizé are young (16–35), and come from many countries and faith backgrounds. The ecumenical success of Taizé is due largely in part to the care and dedication with which the music is prepared for the liturgy. The community's reflections on the liturgy and the music itself are readily available and provide an important practical resource for churches.

2) The World Council of Churches has done pioneering work in opening up the riches of the music of non-Western cultures. The churches of Africa and Asia are the crucibles of Christianity in the next century, and there is much in their musical traditions which will help us. Although we may not recreate the actual music, we have much to learn about the relationship of music to the sacred. We may have to look with considerable humility at these traditions and recognize that Western European culture has given up much of its soul as its music lost its base in the community. The WCC publications are available world-wide.

3) The Iona Community is a community which has made the ancient abbey on Iona the focus of their movement to bring renewal to the churches of Great Britain. The members have worked for the renewal of the liturgy in the reformed tradition. Their musical resources provide an example of creativity within a particular tradition which has opened itself up to ecumenical influence. Their song-books are widely available.

4) Although the Orff method is primarily a teaching method, its principles are invaluable musical support for the liturgy. The German composer, Carl Orff, pioneered the method after despairing that his musical students would ever internalize their music in a holistic way, uniting both the physical and the spiritual. His method encourages children and adults to recapture music for themselves. The use of repeated rhythms and melodies makes the music readily accessible. More importantly, Orff saw every child as a composer, as a music creator, as well as a music maker. The method allows for extraordinary flights of creativity and can be a fruitful core for the music of the liturgy. Many Orff teachers would be interested in such an experiment.

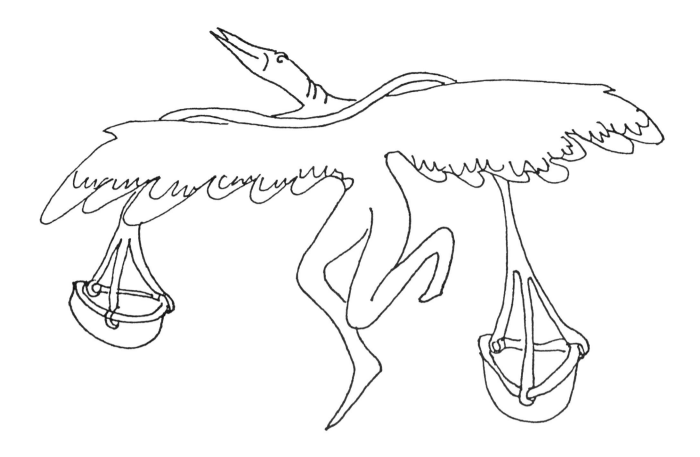

Evaluation

"I think the music is terrific! It really makes me feel like singing." I didn't know church could be outside." "Sometimes it is hard to hear what people are saying, especially the readers. We need a sound system." "It really helps when there are posters on the wall to explain the idea of the readings." "I like having real bread." "I prefer wafers." "I have trouble with the wine. It's very sour."

These comments were all made at one of our evaluation sessions. We held this in June, just before the summer holidays, to give the congregation a chance to say what they liked and what could be improved in the liturgies they had experienced. Joseph Gelineau distinguishes between the congregation which comes to worship and the community which plans liturgy for the congregation. Not everyone can be expected to invest the amount of energy required to be a member of a community. Many will be content with being members of the congregation. However, there should be opportunity for everyone to evaluate the experiences of worship in which they have participated.

When we first planned this event, we linked it with a barbecue on a week-day evening. Sharing a meal together created an informal and friendly atmosphere in which we could speak honestly and openly to each other when we got down to the business of evaluation. We also expected that attendance would be limited to the faithful few, and so provided a written form on the previous Sunday for the majority to make their comments. We were mistaken about the degree of interest in the evaluation session, but the form still proved to be useful.

We particularly encouraged the attendance of children at the barbecue and evaluation session. After our meal we all sat around in a circle with the children in the centre. One of the leaders interviewed them with simple questions about what they liked and what ideas they had for improvement, making sure that their comments could be heard by the adults and teenagers. In order to jog their memories of 10 months of liturgies, we had on display the various artifacts and visual creations from the past year. Children tend to come right to the point without wasting time. Their suggestions for improvement are usually concrete. This session was also an invaluable time for learning how and to what extent they were engaged in the action of worship.

Ten to 15 minutes is usually the limit to their patience for this exercise, and so the children were excused to the nearby park while the adults and teenagers had their opportunity for evaluation.

We normally choose a chairperson outside the planning team so that people feel they can speak freely if they have critical comments to make. The topics covered are the same as those on the written form. We also appoint a recorder who summarizes the meeting and makes a written report available to the whole congregation.

The evaluation session is an opportunity for expressing creative ideas. Some of these the planning team will take and use. However, most often the person with the idea is the one best suited to implement it, and so if there are no major obstructions we try to assign responsibilities then and there for next steps. We still don't have a permanent sound system and the pews are still in place; but on the other hand, the sermons have improved, we are incorporating languages other than English, and as one person remarked, "Being invited to contribute in specific ways makes one really part of the community."

Here is an example of the form which we use and adapt each year for gathering evaluations.

* * *

EVALUATION OF THE FOLK MASS

(People are invited to participate in the evaluation process by writing their comments and attending the session. The names of the planners for the year are listed.)

Planning Principles

1. That all members of the congregation feel included and engaged in worship. There will be a special attempt to include children and young people.
2. That people's diverse backgrounds, origins, and characteristics will be honoured. That people will have the opportunity to participate in an inclusive but non-coercive community.
3. To seek a lively and revitalized style of worship that remains within and draws upon the strengths of the catholic tradition.
4. To use music that draws upon a variety of folk traditions from around the world (African, Latin American, English, Celtic, French, North American).
5. To develop liturgy that incorporates concern for local and global issues within a context of Christian hope.
6. To communicate clearly and enable participation through a comprehensive printed leaflet.
7. To identify and enable the exercise of particular gifts of ministry within the context of worship and social gathering.

In your view have these principles been evident in the liturgies you have attended? Which have been realized? What suggestions would you have for improvement?

We would appreciate your comments on the following questions:

SPACE. Were the liturgies in the most appropriate spaces available? How was the sound and the lighting? Do you have any suggestions for a better use of space?

LEADERSHIP. Do the presiders encourage celebration? Any comments on the homilies?

MUSIC. Does the music make you feel like singing? Are the musicians performing or leading?

VISUAL IMPACT. Do the actions of the liturgy come across clearly? Do the liturgical symbols and artistic creations communicate well?

COMMUNITY. Do you feel welcome and happy to be there? Whom are we including and whom are we excluding?

Do you have any comments on specific liturgies? Does anything in particular stand out in your memory?

Would you like to volunteer for any aspect of the folk mass?

* * *

The final word goes to some of the comments which emerged from our evaluations: "This is the only service anywhere that my children willingly attend. At St. Mary's we are allowed to have ideas."

Bibliography

As we have tried to indicate in the course of this book, our liturgical ideas have come from many sources: first of all the scriptures, then the great variety of people who gather together for worship in our parish, other liturgies we have attended, contemporary movies and music, and all the symbols imbedded in the culture by which we define our lives. Occasionally we have learned something from a book, and so here is a brief selection.

Cavalletti, Sofia. *The Religious Potential of the Child.* Paulist Press, 1983. Cavalletti is a disciple of Maria Montessori and translated this famous educator's principles into the sphere of spiritual education. She describes her book as "a document of the child's spiritual and religious capacities."

Dillistone, F.W. *The Power of Symbols*. SCM Press, 1986. For the more theoretically inclined, a luminous book on the subject of symbolism. "To live symbolically spells true freedom."

Gelineau, Joseph. *The Liturgy Today and Tomorrow*. Darton, Longman and Todd, 1978. Reflections on the essentials of liturgy and the reforms of Vatican II from a famous French Roman Catholic. His insights are ecumenical and international.

Green, Robin. *Only Connect*. Darton, Longman and Todd, 1987. "Worship and liturgy from the perspective of pastoral care" by an English priest who makes extensive use of his experience in psychotherapy and Jungian psychology.

Liturgy. Quarterly Journal of the Liturgical Conference. Each issue is the size of a small book and contains a mix of theory and practice. Back issues are available.

Nelson, Gertrud Mueller. *To Dance with God*. Paulist Press, 1986. Subtitled "Family Ritual and Community Celebration," this book is creative both in its treatment of ritual and in its many practical ideas.

Primavesi, Anne and Henderson, Jennifer. *Our God Has No Favourites*. Resource Publications, 1989. This book is written from the crucible of Northern Ireland and is described as a liberation theology of the eucharist. The revolutionary nature of the eucharist is kept before us with simplicity and compassion.

Schaffran, Janet and Kozak, Pat. *More Than Words*. Meyer Stone Books, 1988. A good resource book of prayer and ritual for inclusive communities which can be used by both radical and conservative Christians (with discretion).

Music Resources

The following list is intended as a starting point for liturgical planners. Contemporary liturgical music easily crosses denominational boundaries, and planners should be adventuresome and experience what other traditions and communities of faith have to offer.

Batastini, R. et al. (eds). *Worship*. 3rd edition. G.I.A. Publications, 1970.

Bell, J. and G. Maule (eds). *Iona Community: Wild Goose Songs*. 3 vols. Wild Goose

Publications, 1987.

Berthier, J. *Music from Taizé.* 2 vols. G.I.A. Publications, 1982.

Berthier, J. *Songs and Prayers from Taizé.* Geoffrey Chapman Mowbray, 1991.

Boulton Smith, G. (ed). *Music for the Mass.* Geoffrey Chapman, 1985.

Glory and Praise: Parish Music Program. North American Liturgy Resources, 1984.

Haas, D. *Who Calls You by Name.* G.I.A. Publications, 1984.

Haugen, M. *Shepherd Me, O God* G.I.A. Publications, 1987.

Hobbs, R. (ed). *Songs for a Gospel People.* Wood Lake Books, 1987.

Jesus Christ — The Life of the World World Council of Churches, 1987.

Loh, I. (ed). *African Songs of Worship.* World Council of Churches, 1986.

Mims, G. (ed). *Songs for Celebration.* Church Hymnal Corporation, 1980.

North American Liturgy Resources. North American Liturgy Resources and G.I.A. Publications, 1988.